By G.C.

GRANDMOTHER'S STORIES

GRANDMOTHER'S STORIES

BY

GRACE CLEMENSON

YE GALLEON PRESS
FAIRFIELD, WASHINGTON

Library of Congress Cataloging-in-Publication Data

Clemenson, Grace. 1916-
    Grandmother's stories / by Grace Clemenson.
    p. cm.
    ISBN 0-87770-492-9
    1. Clemenson, Grace, 1916- . 2. Minnesota — Biography. 3. Iowa — Biography. 4 Pioneers — Minnesota — Biography. I. Title.
CT275.C6427A3   1991   977.6'05'092—dc20   91-9286
                                                                                                                  [B]

Copyright © Grace Clemenson
Spokane, Washington
1991

GRANDMOTHER'S STORIES

DEDICATION:

Grandmother's Stories For My Grandchildren:

In Fondest Memory of My Mother:

This is my life story. Writing this has not been an easy task, but a rewarding one and immensely exciting and enjoyable.

As one sits down to recall the past, many pictures come into view. One has to decide which to put first, what comes second, how to begin and how to end.

My grandchildren, this is for you.

Grace Johnston Clemenson

GRACE CLEMENSON

Daddy and me out for a dog cart ride taken on the Tamrack River in Norden, Minnesota.

Mother and me in Mother's log cabin on the Tamrack River in Norden, Minnesota.

GRANDMOTHER'S STORIES

MY BABY DAYS IN THE LOG CABIN.

My grandchildren, this is for you. I know you will love it, just because it is part of the past and it is Grandmother's own story. My earliest years up until I was three years old were spent on my mother's homestead in northern Minnesota on the banks of the Tamarack River. Mother had a cozy log cabin there, and this is the home she and my father brought me to when I was about two weeks old. I do not remember the cabin, but I have a picture of the inside of it, which reflects the talents and homemaking abilities of my dear mother.

I was born in a tent, and this was unusual even for the year of 1916. My entry into the world came about in this way. My mother and father were thrilled when they realized I was on my way. Being their first-born, they wanted nothing but the best. They lived twenty miles from the doctor, and my father said he must somehow provide a doctor for this event, so he planned that since he could not bring the doctor to us, he would take us to the doctor. He bought a tent, locked up the cabin door, put us all in the wagon, and took us to Bemidji, the county seat of Beltrimi County.

It was the month of June. The birds were singing and the flowers blooming when we started out. It was a full day's journey to our campsite on the beautiful shores of Lake Bemidji. When we arrived, my daddy pitched the tent, put a floor in it, and we settled down to wait. The spot he chose for our campsite was on Diamond Point. The birds sang in the trees, and the days were hot and sunny. The waters on Lake Bemidji were glittering and shimmering in the sunshine. My daddy spent his time swimming and diving. Once he dived for a clam and brought up a large live shell. On opening it he found a pure and shining pearl. My mother wrapped it in cotton and put it into her little square tin keepsake box. For years, as we were growing up. we would be allowed from time to time to take out the pearl and hold it while we listened to the story again and again. Finally with too many fingers touching and grasping, the pearl was lost.

We had a friend we called Nurse Smith. She was the best, they said, having had much experience in the hospitals in France during the early days of World War I. As my mother's time drew near, Nurse Smith came to stay with us. The third day of July, 1916, I arrived with great haste, and although my daddy hurried off for the doctor, I managed to arrive before he did. This left Nurse Smith with the honor of bringing me into the world. What joy! A perfectly formed baby girl! They named me Minnie Grace for my maternal and paternal grandmothers. After the proper two weeks of laying in, my mother was allowed to get up, and was soon able to travel. My daddy folded up the tent, packed me into a clothes basket, and we all got into the wagon and rode back to our log cabin home.

This was a wild country. Wolves, bears, deer, moose, bobcats, lynx, weasles, skunks, rabbits, and porcupines all roamed the woods and stalked the night. On many occasions we had reason to fear. One time, my mother came into my bedroom where I had been crying. She was shocked to see several hungry weasles sitting on the windowsill outside my window. They were watching me and contemplating a noon-time meal.

While we lived in this cabin, two more babies were born with the gentle help of our dear Nurse Smith. My sister Crystal Mae was born on June twenty-first of nineteen seventeen on the brightest day of the year. Vern was born on September twelfth of nineteen eighteen. When I was about three years old we moved. My daddy bought a piece of lakeshore property on the south shore of Red Lake. We went to live in another log cabin. This cabin had three rooms. One main room with two windows facing the lake. It was heated with an oil drum, wood-burning heater. A lean-to kitchen was heated with a woodburning cook stove. One big bedroom had no heat.

Now I began to see, remember, and to take note of what was going on around me. The winters were long and bitterly cold. How well I remember the long, red flannel night gowns my mother made for Crystal and me to wear on those cold winter nights. The stars and the moon shone bright as day as they reflected on the snow. The eerie blood curdling cries of the wolves in the timber around our cabin sent frightening chills through and through us. We were thankful to be safe in our cozy, warm beds. Sweet dreams soon overcame us.

One cold, winter day as Crystal, Vern, and I were watching the frozen lake from the window, two horses pulling a sled came into our view. The sled stopped in front of our house, and two families of Indians got out.

"Indians! Mother, Indians are coming!" we shouted. Squaws, papooses, children, and bucks pushed the door open and came crowding into our little kitchen. They were from the Chipawa Indian Reservation near us.

A baby was crying. As my mother stood looking at them in amazement, the father said, "Sick papoose." Mother found a diaper and a blanket. She changed the baby and wrapped him up. She heated a bottle of milk, then opened the oven door and sat down in front of it, feeding the baby the warm milk from the bottle. Soon the baby fell asleep. Crystal, Vern and I passed out cookies and milk to the children and squaws. They ate cookies as they stood around chattering to each other in Chipawa. Soon everyone was warm, and with the baby still sleeping, they left. As

GRANDMOTHER'S STORIES

we watched out the window, we saw a man coming back. He carried something in his hand. He pushed open the door and handed my mother a paper bag. We crowded around, anxious to open it. We found it half full of Indian corn. This was their gift of thank you to us for our hospitality. It was *all* they had to give. We watched them as they drove away in the cold. We were thankful for our cozy, warm cabin and for cookies and milk.

Grace and Crystal licking out the cake pan. Homestead days on the Tamrack River.

Grace and Crystal turning the ice cream freezer in Norden, Minnesota.

GRACE CLEMENSON

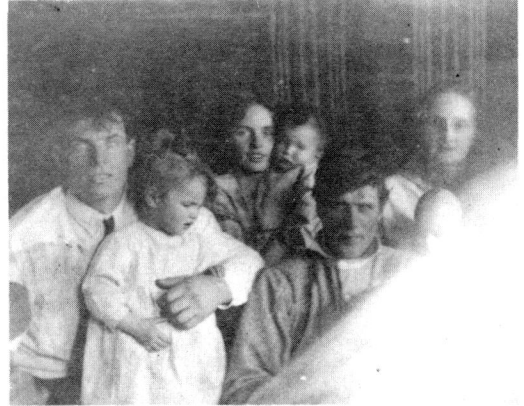

John Halverson, his wife Laura, Wanda and Ruth.

Uncle John Halverson holding Wanda, Aunt Laura holding Ruth. Mary and George Johnston, 1918.

Mary Maynard, Laura Maynard, with Father Champ Maynard. Homestead Day on the Tamrack River, 1913-1914.

GRANDMOTHER'S STORIES

CHRISTMAS IN THE LOG CABIN

Christmas was the bright spot in the dark and dreary winters. The excitement and mystery of it all cannot be described. The mystery was in the form of Santa Claus with his eight reindeer galloping through the air. Old Santa himself came slipping silently down the chimney. How could he find our house tucked away in this frozen, out-of-the-way spot in the great big world? This was another mystery to me. The social event of the winter was the school Christmas program. This took place a week before Christmas. Crystal and I were still too young to go to school. Still the teacher told us that if we would learn a poem we could be in the Christmas program. How well I remember the matching red wool jumpers and white blouses Mother made for us one year for this occasion. Our mail order shoes, ordered from the Savage catalog, did not come on time. Mother cut out little leather moccasins and sewed and trimmed them with red yarn to match the jumpers. These we wore to the Christmas program. The schoolhouse was brightly trimmed with red and green streamers strung along the ceiling. A huge tree stood in one corner, dressed in tinsel and strings of popcorn. Little candles were fastened on the boughs. Underneath the tree stood a big box of apples and sacks of Christmas candy. After our verses were said and the program was over, the candles on the tree were lit, Santa Claus came in with his bag of gifts. Candy and the apples were passed out. Following this came visiting time for the parents, and play time for the children. Late in the evening we began our long ride home in the sled. The horses carried us along fast, as they were cold and anxious to get into their warm barn. We were tucked warm in the hay. Jack Frost nipped at our noses as we sailed along, watching the stars and listening to the jingle of the horses' harness.

At home we began our preparation for our own home Christmas. First, there was the baking and the candy making. Then the house was cleaned and scrubbed spotless. On Christmas Eve day we all dressed in our warm outdoor clothes, for this was the day to go hunting for our Christmas tree. We all got into the sled. With horses pulling, we rode through the snow, and into the woods. After a long ride and careful searching, we finally found just the right tree. At home, daddy set the tree up in a corner of our living room. We all helped put on the decorations. Then we got out our homemade gifts which we had wrapped and carefully hidden away. When the gifts were in place, we were ready for our supper. Mother had a kettle of bean soup cooking all afternoon, and we smelled fresh corn bread coming from the oven. We were hungry now, and ate heartily. After the meal was over and the kitchen was tidied up, we went into the living room and sat around the tree. Daddy lit the candles. We opened our gifts to one another. After our gift exchange was over and the excitement died down, daddy told us that it was time to hang up our stockings and go to bed. On a small table near the tree we left cookies and milk for Santa Claus. Now we were hurried off to bed. We waited for sleep that did not come. I listened to strange noises around the tree, and thought that Santa must surely be there. I closed my eyes tight. In a minute I was asleep. Suddenly I was awakened by a shout. "Merry Christmas! Santa Claus has been here!" At last the great day had arrived. I got up in a daze and looked around. I glanced at the little table. Yes, the cookies and milk were gone. Santa never failed us. Best of all, he came with an abundance of the best. He left dolls, tea sets, books, blocks, drums, sleds, nuts, candy, apples, and best of all, an orange in the tip of every stocking. I discovered as I grew up that my daddy's well-to-do relatives in St. Louis and Minneapolis were Santa's most active helpers.

Another Christmas stands out in my mind. That was the year of the Christmas tree fire. Uncle John and Aunt Laura and their five children, Wanda, Ruth, Sheila, Maxine and Alice, who was the baby, came for Christmas. They came many miles in a covered sleigh, a two-days' journey from their home in Gonvick. They brought their gifts and a paper Santa Claus. How well I remember the excitement on Chirstmas Eve Day. Daddy and Uncle John said that we must all get dressed in our outdoor clothes for we were going to the woods to hunt for a Christmas tree. We all went, Wanda, Ruth, Sheila, Maxine, Vern, Crystal and Me. I remember that Grandpa Champ also decided to ride along. We had quite a sleigh load. I wondered where we would put the tree.

We found a small nicely shaped little spruce. Everyone agreed that it was just the right one. The rest of the day was spent setting up the tree and putting on the decorations. Mother and Aunt Laura put on the tinsel, popcorn strings and icicles. Each child was given an ornament to put in place. Mine was a gold star made of card board with a string attached. I hung it carefully on a lower branch.

Last of all the candles were fastened on. They were tiny wax candles set into a holder which was snapped onto the branches. The paper santa clause was hung on the wall beside the tree. Gifts were arranged under the tree. Now we were ready for the lighting of the candles.

We all sat down on the floor, admiring the tree and watching daddy as he lit the candles. One by one they began to shine, emitting a soft glow to the room. Suddenly the paper santa clause came down. It fell against a lighted candle. Everything began to burn. The blaze spread fast. Uncle John and daddy jumped up and doused the tree with pails of water which they kept on hand in one corner of the room. We received many soggy gifts. I do not remember any dampened spirits.

GRANDMOTHER'S STORIES

After the holidays winter sent in with a vengeance. Cold winds blew across the lake from the north. Our little log cabin stood firm and strong under the icy blasts. Inches of frost covered the windows, so we could no longer see out. Storm windows and storm doors were unheard of. We awoke on many frigid mornings to find our cabin door frozen shut. Mother would heat a teakettle of water and pour under the door, and with a little pushing and shoving she would get it open. A shovel was a necessary tool to keep in the house in winter. Mother would then take the shovel and shovel out. The water in the water pail froze into a cake of ice. The food in the cupboard froze. My mother built a fire in the heater and the cookstove. Soon she had the house warm and the pancake griddle hot. When we heard the beating of the pancake batter we knew it was time to get up. We jumped out of our warm beds and ran for the heater. There we dressed; standing as near the stove as possible. We pulled on our wool underwear and socks. With our clothing on, our teeth brushed, faces washed and hair combed we were ready for breakfast.

God's woodland creatures felt the cold, too. One morning as my daddy was dressing he felt a warm furry ball on the back of his neck. He reached back and pulled out a little mouse that had found a warm nest in his long johns. The mouse jumped and leaped across the room and found another warm spot behind the woodbox near the cook stove.

My Mother, Mary Maynard Johnston, Homestead Days on the Tamrack River, Norden, Minnesota, about 1913.

The Johnstons; Mother, Daddy, Crystal, Vern, Grace, and Elsie in Shotley, Minnesota.

GRACE CLEMENSON

Vern, Crystal, Mother, Elsie and Grace Johnston on Red Lake in Shotley, Minnesota.

The Johnstons in 1924. Grace, Vern, Daddy, Mother, Crystal and Elsie in Shotley, Minnesota.

Vivian and Vern Maynard. Mary Maynard Johnston, Champ Maynard, Mildred Maynard, Crystal and Elsie Johnston.

GRANDMOTHER'S STORIES

MY HOME IN THE CITY:

I was four years old on July third of nineteen twenty. In the fall of nineteen twenty we had an outbreak of scarlet fever in our community. Crystal, Vern, Ruth, our hired girl, and I were all sick at the same time. We were all put to bed, each on our own cot, in our own corner of the big lean-to bedroom. Sore throats, high temperatures, vomiting, headaches, and finally breaking out in a bright red rash were the symptoms of scarlet fever. It was a ravaging disease. It affects the eyes, ears, and the kidneys. It was the cause of many deaths in our community. Mother was our only doctor. She studied the big black doctor book very diligently. The counsel was to feed a cold and starve a fever. This she believed saved our lives.

Dr. Bone, our only country doctor, had his office in Kelliher, twenty miles distant. He was summoned at the onset of our illness. We were the last to see him. His mode of travel was by horse and sleigh. Other families along the way were also in need of his help. Dr. Bone made many stops and ate with his friends along the way. He slept in a bed of straw in the bottom of the sleigh which a teamster drove from home to home. Ruth, Crystal, and Vern were all recovered when he reached our house. I was still in bed. Following scarlet fever, rheumatic fever set in. I was suffering aches and pains in all of my joints. My kidneys were affected. My ears were draining. My heart was weakened and I was temporarily blind.

How well I remember the excitement of that spring day. Dr. Bone was coming to see me. He examined me and gave my mother the orders. I must go to the University Hospital in Minneapolis. Ruth, our hired girl, was elected to take me on the train. We spent several days packing and getting ready for the trip. I was very excited of course, not knowing of the new world I would be entering or how homesick I would be. I said, good-by to my mother and Crystal and Vern. Daddy took Ruth and me to the train depot in Kelliher. The train left at seven o'clock in the morning and arrived in Minneapolis at seven o'clock in the evening. Aunt Jenny was there to meet us and took me to her house.

Aunt Jenny's home was a well-to-do city dwelling on Blasedell Avenue. There was central heating and lighting and a bath tub with hot and cold running water. There was an ice box and a gas cooking stove. This was a new and strange life style for me. I did not like it. I was frightened and homesick. When they wanted me to jump into a tub of running water, my fears took control and I fought. When they tried to get me to take a nap, I ran away.

I was an out-patient at the University Hospital. My first encounter with a doctor was an unhappy one for him. The examination of my eyes, nose and throat was a battle and a disaster. I scratched, kicked and bit. The doctor spanked me. My dear, understanding aunt would not put up with this. She marched me out of his office, reported him to the superintendent, and ordered another doctor for me. I was taken home and I proclaimed myself to be the winner of the day's battles. Several days later my aunt and I went back to see a new doctor. He was gentle and kind, a lover of children. I fell in love with him. He helped me overcome my fears, and soon he was able to work with me. He gave me a complete physical and prescribed my treatment. The medication for my draining ears was three drops of alcohol and boric acid in each ear three times daily. The pain was excruciating. I kicked and screamed. Aunt Jenny was patient and used tact in her handling of me. I learned to bear the pain and bravely put my head on the pillow while she administered the medication.

Street cars were noisy, rattly contraptions. They ran on a track carrying passengers. They had a set of cymbals which the conductor operated with his foot and could clang in case of danger. A bell hung up in front of the window. The conductor kept it ringing just to let people know he was coming. One day as I was left alone at a friend's house, I watched the street cars go by. I began to get some interesting thoughts. I wondered what the conductor would do if I stopped his street car. I could do it if I just went out and sat down on the track. This I did. The conductor saw me in time to get his foot on the cymbals and began his clanging. His right hand got hold of the bell rope. The bell began to ring. This was exciting. I sat there very still, curious and unafraid. The street car came up to me and stopped. What would happen now? The conductor stepped out, took me up gently in his arms and set me down carefully on the porch. Then he gave me a gentle smile. Without a word he stepped back into his car and with the bell ringing, he drove away. I sat there in amazement, feeling very comforted. I had challenged the world and the world has responded with kindness.

My city life began to take on a whole new meaning. I was no longer homesick or afraid. I had forgotten my log cabin home. My aunt was very busy with social activities. She was an active member of the Daughters of the American Revolution. She attended luncheons, theaters and operas. Many times I was allowed to accompany her. I was dressed in a whole new fashionable wardrobe. I wore a navy blue coat with white collar and cuffs and a bonnet to match. White knee socks and black patent leather slippers, ribbons in my hair and tiny white gloves completed my wardrobe. In all of these I felt very comfortable and happy.

How well I remember my fifth birthday on July 3rd of nineteen-twenty-one. On Sunday, Aunt Jenny, my cousin Jane and I attended Sunday School and church.

GRANDMOTHER'S STORIES

I loved my Sunday School class and my teacher. I walked into the room and sat down in my chair. After the opening songs were sung and the prayer was said the teacher asked, "Do you know whose birthday it is today?" No one answered, so she said, "Grace is five years old today, and we have a little cake with five candles." She brought out the cake and lit the candles. While we watched the candles burn, the children sang "Happy Birthday." This was another new experience for me and a pleasant one at that.

At home after church Dr. and Mrs. McGill and their daughter Ariel, came for dinner. Again there was cake with candles and gifts to open. In the afternoon, Aunt Jenny and I went for a ride in Dr. McGill's new car. It was very different from the cars of today. I do remember that it was built up high off the ground, and we had to step up on a running board to get in. Dr. McGill lifted me up into the seat. Aunt Jenny stepped on the running board and Dr. McGill held her arm to steady her until she was seated. The seats were hard and covered with black leather decorated with a gold colored braid. When we were all seated, Dr. McGill took out the iron crank and walked to the front of the car. He put the crank in place and gave it a few hard turns. The motor roared and sputtered, Dr. McGill jumped in. He adjusted the clutch, pushed up the gas lever, and we were off with a jerk. Smoke and dust came billowing out behind us. The sun was shining brightly and I complained that the light was hurting my eyes. Dr. McGill stopped the car and pulled down the shade on my window. I was impressed with his thoughtfulness, and I felt very happy.

We drove for some time. I wondered where we were going. We were out in the country now. Suddenly we stopped with a jerk. We all got out. There in front of us was a huge waterfall. I was told that this was St. Anthony Falls. There was no park there at this time, we walked around through the grass and weeds. I stared up at the falls, feeling the mist on my face as it poured gallons of water at my feet. The grown-ups stood looking up in silence, each one engrossed in his own thoughts. It was awesome — a beautiful sight and a little bit frightening to me. Soon we departed for the drive home. This was a memorable day for me. One which I still remember. Dr. and Mrs. McGill wanted to adopt me. They wrote a letter to my parents presenting this offer to them. Their answer was "No." They wanted me back. I knew nothing of this at the time. My mother told me about it in later years.

One day Aunt Jenny told me that we would soon be taking our vacation. This was a new word to me and I wondered what was going to happen next. Soon my cousin Ralph came for us in an old Model T Ford, better known as the "Tin Lizzie." He told us to hurry and get in as he had to leave at once and get back to the farm. So this was it — a vacation on the farm. We all got in, Aunt Jenny and Ralph in the front seat and Jane and I in the back, squeezed around suitcases and boxes. Jane was seven years older that I, and was very bossy. I did not cooperate with her and we had our fights. The back seat ride gave us ample time to vent our differences. We rode all day. At about five o'clock we arrived at the farm. Uncle John was there to meet us. After the greetings were said, Jane and I began to look around. We heard some cows bawling, and Uncle John said they were sad because he had taken their calves away from them that day. Then we saw the big red bull snorting and pawing the ground. Jane said to me, "I am going to put you on the bull's back." I was frightened and angry and with my fist I hit her in the stomach. She doubled up and went crying to the house. I followed a long way behind because I felt sure that this time I would get my punishment. I heard Jane say, "Grace punched me in the stomach." Aunt Jenny said, "Well, if you didn't tease her all the time you wouldn't get hurt." I walked into the kitchen then feeling a little smug. Jane kept on crying. Just then Uncle John came into the kitchen carrying a pail full of eggs. He took one egg in his hand and put it up to Jane's ear. Then he put his other hand to her other ear and pretended to take an egg out. "See," he said, "this egg went through your head, in one ear and out the other." We knew it was a trick, but we laughed and were happy again.

It was at the farm that I had my first encounter with a telephone. The telephone in those days was made up of a huge wooden box with a mouth piece fastened to the front. On the left side fastened to a cord was the ear piece. On the right side was a crank which could be turned for ringing the proper longs and shorts. This whole contraption was hung on the wall in the kitchen. One evening after supper the telephone rang. Uncle John picked up the ear piece and listened. Then he shouted, "Hello! You old bellyacher." His neighbor on the other end of the line shouted back. The conversation continued loud and noisy with many name-callings. I looked at Jane and Jane looked at me. We sometimes did some funny name-calling, too, I wondered if she was wishing that I lived on a nearby farm so she could talk to me on the phone.

One day this city life came to an end. Aunt Jenny said to me. "The time has come for you to go back to your log cabin home. You will live again with your mother and daddy and Crystal and Vern," Aunt Jenny packed all my fine clothes and soon we were seated on the train going north to the little lumberjack town of Kelliher. We passed several log cabins along the way and Aunt Jenny would say to me, "See that shack? That is where you will be living." I would get angry and say, "No, it isn't. That's not true." I thought she was teasing me. Now I know that she was preparing me for a rude awakening. That evening we came to Kelliher, the end of the line. My mother and father were there to meet me. I remember how happy

GRANDMOTHER'S STORIES

they looked and they kept smiling at me. To me they looked like strangers and I could not return their smiles. I hung on to my Aunt Jenny's hand and insisted on spending the night with her in the hotel. The next morning I had to say goodby to Aunt Jenny. She boarded the train for the all day trip back to Minneapolis. I waived as the whistle blew a long, lonely call. Puffs of black smoke circled into the air, and the train disappeared down the track. I felt sad and alone. I looked around and there were my parents, smiling at me. They took hold of my hand and led me to a wagon which they said we would be riding in. Daddy hitched two horses to their singletrees and fastened the tongue of the wagon in place. We all got up on the high seat, and with a flick of the reins we were off, bumping and joggling over the muddy road. I felt strange and unhappy. This couldn't be me. We jostled along in the wagon for twenty miles. Finally my daddy said, "We're home." He smiled as he lifted me down from the wagon. I didn't feel like smiling. The first thing I saw was Crystal and Vern playing in the mud. They were making mud pies. They had mud on their faces and mud in their hair. They were bare-foot, and mud oozed between their toes. Crystal had on a long shift dress and mud streaked down the front. "No." I said to myself, "this is not my kind of living." I stayed in the house for many days and refused to go out and play. The adjustment back to my log cabin home was slow and painful.

Ruth Knutson, Grace, Mother, Vern, Chrystal Johnston, Nibs, our dog, Peggy Jane, our doll, in Shotley, Minnesota on Red Lake.

GRACE CLEMENSON

George Henry Johnston and Mary Edith Maynard, married Dec. 2, 1914.

John Obed Halvorson and Laura Aurora Halvorson, married Dec. 2, 1914.

GRANDMOTHER'S STORIES

GRANDPA PETER JOHNSTON

My Grandfather Johnston, who was deaf and blind, came to live with us. He came on the train from Minneapolis. We met him at the station and brought him home by horse and buggy. He had been living with Aunt Jenny. It became my job again, as in the city, to take him out for his daily walk. I took hold of his hand and we shuffled slowly around the yard. It became a very boring job and to liven things up a bit I led him up to the side of the house and let go of his hand. I stepped back and watched to see what he would do. With his black gold-headed cane he tapped the side of the wall. With his free hand he began to feel his way to the corner. As he stood at the corner, a cat came running wildly around the house and close behind came our barking dog. Grandpa stood firm, leaning on his cane. I ran up to him, then, feeling a little frightened. I took him by the hand and led him away to safety. Grandpa and I kept our little secret and my mother never knew of my naughty act.

Grandpa told us stories about a boy named Tommy and a girl named Kitty. Tommy and Kitty had many exciting adventures and we heard them all. Grandpa sang to us songs of the Civil War and old hymns from his childhood as he rocked us in his old rocking chair. Grandpa was careful about his table grace and evening prayers. How well I remember seeing him at bedtimes, just as the sun was setting in the West, kneeling by his bed in prayer. Always, he repeated the Lord's Prayer out loud, very slowly. Many times I stood in his bedroom door and watched and listened. Now as I grow older I find myself following his example.

Peter Johnston was born in Ogdensburg, New York. His mother was Sally Livingston and his Father was Benjamin Johnston. They were of English and Scotch descent. Grandpa Johnston was born in eighteen thirty six and died in nineteen twenty five at the age of eighty-nine. Grandpa's father, Benjamin, was strict and stern and demanded much hard work of young Peter. One fourth of July when Peter was fourteen years old, he was hoeing potatoes in his father's garden. There was a celebration in town that day, but young Peter was not allowed to go. Friends and neighbors drove by in their horse-drawn buggies on their way to the town's celebration. Peter heard one of them say "Poor boy. He has to hoe potatoes on the Fourth of July." Peter threw down his hoe and ran away. He went into town to the celebration, and from there he kept going, out into an unknown world. He never again returned to his home in New York, and never again did he see his father and mother. Peter worked his way west to Aurora, Illinois, where he began farming. At the age of twenty-five he enlisted in the Civil War. He served four years until the close. He was in the battle of Pea Ridge, Perryville and Stone River. He was present at the famous Douglas-Lincoln debate.

While Peter was in the Civil War he met a young man by the name of George Merrill. They became best buddies. George was wounded in battle and it was Peter who took him to his home in Iowa. Peter stayed there in George's home and nursed him back to health. George had a sister Grace who soon caught the eye of young Peter. They were married in 1865. Peter was twenty-nine years old when he married and he and Grace were married for thirty-two years. They had four children, Jenny, Ben, George and a baby who died in infancy. Jenny was twenty years old when George was born.

During these years Peter studied law. In 1882 he moved his family to Estherville, Iowa, where he began a very successful law practice. Peter was a loyal Democrat, and on entering the newspaper business he became the founder and editor of the *Estherville Democrat*. Peter was postmaster of Estherville under Grover Cleveland. After years of study and proof-reading, Peter's eyes began to give out. He had an eye operation at the hospital in Iowa City, Iowa and was given strict instuctions to give up his reading and rest his eyes. This he refused to do. Finally he became blind. He lost his hearing, too, as a result of a war injury. When he lived with us he was both deaf and blind. He died on April eighth of nineteen twenty-five, in his room in our home. The date of his death was the anniversary of Lee's surrender.

How well I remember the day of his death. I was nine years old, and Crystal and I had been in school all day. After a mile-and-a-half walk we reached home at about five o'clock. Mother met us at the door. "Grandpa died today," she said and threw her apron over her face and cried. We were startled and sorry. We did not often see our mother crying.

Crystal and I could not feel the sorrow displayed around us. We were young and strange things were taking place in our home. We were caught in the excitement of it all. Neighbors came in with food, and our kind neighbor woman, Mrs. Urseth made a bouquet of paper flowers for the casket. The undertaker came and performed his duties while we were sent out doors to play. The casket was brought out from Kelliher, twenty miles distant, by horse and wagon. Mother was busy dyeing burlap gunny sacks in a big pot of green dye. She cut them and sewed them into drapes for our living room window. We did not go to school for several days.

The day of the funeral arrived. The minister came from Kelliher. Neighbors came in horse and buggy. The casket was set in the center of the living room, and chairs were placed around it. As the minister preached we all sat looking at the casket. When the service was over, daddy came and lifted me up so I could look down at grandpa's face. He looked beautiful with his white hair and beard and his long, slender hands folded on his breast. Daddy said, "Say good-by to Grandpa now, for you will never see him again. I gazed into his face with love but the tears did not come. Soon after this the casket was closed, put into the back of our wagon and taken to Kelliher. At Kelliher it was put on the train and taken to Minneapolis. At Minneapolis there was a change of trains, with my daddy still accompanying it, the casket was taken to Estherville, Iowa. Grandpa was buried there beside my grandmother, Grace. "Our Father which art in Heaven, hallowed be thy name." The Lord's Prayer, which my grandfather prayed every evening before bedtime, was silenced in our home forever.

Resting place of Grace Merrill Johnston, died Feb. 12, 1897 and Peter Johnston, died April 8, 1925. Oak Hill Cemetery, Esterville, Iowa.

GRACE CLEMENSON

These two pictures are of the home of Grace and Peter Johnston, Estherville, Iowa.

GRANDMOTHER'S STORIES

GRANDPA CHAMP MAYNARD:

Grandpa Champ Maynard was my mother's father. He was born on August 26, 1868, in Grove Lake, Minnesota. His father was Cyrus Maynard, a farmer and a carpenter. His mother was Luthera Adams Tye Maynard. Champ was the only child of this marriage. He had two stepbrothers, Omer and Otis Tye. In 1891, on September twenty-fifth when grandpa was twenty-three years old, he married Minnie Mann. When Cyrus Maynard died and Luthena became a widow, she made her home with Champ and Minnie. Four children were born to this union. Mary, my mother, who was the oldest, Vern, Laura and Buel. Minnie died when Buel was a baby and my mother became the mother of this home. She left school when she was in the fourth grade, became the housekeeper and raised the younger children.

My Grandpa Champ, in his later years, made his home with his children, going from one home to the other and staying several months in each place. How happy we all were when we were told that it would be our turn to house the honored guest and that grandpa would be coming soon. He came in a buggy in the summer and a sleigh in the winter, pulled by a big gray stallion. He carried a big black valise which contained his clothes and all of his worldly belongings. How excited we were when he opened his big suitcase, for there would be candy and gum for us and books to read.

In those days we had no television, radio or telephone. Our greatest entertainment was found in books. Grandpa read his books to us, told us stories and sang songs. He helped us with our afterschool chores. We sawed and chopped wood together to fill our big wood boxes behind the stoves. We fed hay to the sheep and milked the cows. When our work was done, mother had our supper ready. How well I remember the good bean soup and corn bread mother made for us. After supper grandpa would sit down in his favorite rocker and open up one of his new books. So we spent the long winter evenings listening to grandpa read. Grandpa lived to be ninety-eight years old. He died in the Good Samaritan Home in Clearbrook, Minnesota on October twenty-second of nineteen hundred and sixty-six.

GRACE CLEMENSON

Grandpa Champ Maynard.

The Champ Maynard family; Mary, Grandpa Champ, Grandmother Minnie, Vern, Buel and Laura.

Nolie Mann, Minnie Mann Maynard, Either Mann Hart.

Champ Maynard and brother Otis Tye.

GRANDMOTHER'S STORIES

EARLY DAYS ON RED LAKE:

Red Lake is a very large body of fresh water consisting of an upper and lower lake with a deep wide connecting channel. It is located about fifty miles from the Canadian border. We lived on the south shore of the upper lake. There was a thirteen mile expanse of water from our shore to the north shore.

Red Lake was treacherous and unpredictable. Sudden squalls hit unexpectedly in the summer time. If you happened to be out in a boat during one of these storms, you were in danger of capsizing. You were always on the look out for sudden breezes and cloud formations, regardless of how hot and sunny the day may be. The sudden breezes became strong winds in a matter of minutes. Strong winds create high waves and waves became huge in that thirteen mile expanse of water. With the winds came the sudden flashes of lightning streaking across the sky. Rain came down in torrents. The storm has hit like a wild beast. A little boat will rock and roll and disappear under a mountain wave. One must row straight into the wave and go up and over and down, and up and over.

My daddy and I were out in one of these storms one time while setting out fishing nets. I was rowing. Daddy was letting out the net, when suddenly we felt a tug of breeze. This, we knew, was a storm warning. We saw a small black cloud forming. The breeze turned quickly into a strong wind. Daddy pulled the net into the boat. He took the oars from my hands. He told me to lay down in the bottom of the boat. The lightning flashed around us. Rain came down upon us. The little boat glided up and down on the waves. Daddy knew how to row us through. Soon we reached the shore, drenched to the skin. The thunder rumbled and grew weaker in the distance. The lightning ceased. The storm was over. Our fishing trip was over.

"Who Then is This That He Commands even The Wind and The Water and They Obey Him."
Luke 8:25

From the time I can remember until I was in the fourth grade, we lived on the shores of upper Red Lake. The winters were cold, but the summers, beginning in June, were very beautiful. The birds came back from the South and took up their noisy existence in our big front yard. They built their nests in our elm trees, mated, and laid their eggs. Soon came the feeding and training of the baby birds. Mothers and fathers flew to and fro from lawn to nest dropping worms into hungry mouths. When their wings grew stronger, the babies began their flight out of the nest. Mother and father bird chirped and screamed their encouragement. It was a noisy and exciting time. We watched and helped when we could by chasing cats away and replacing baby birds into their nests. The lake water was beginning to warm, and every day we coaxed to go barefoot. My mother always said. "When the oak leaves are as big as a mouse's ears, you can take off your shoes and stockings." Every morning we ran out into the yard to look up into the oak trees. One morning we saw the leaves as big as mouse ears. We took off our shoes and stockings and ran for the lake. Soon after this we put on our swimming suits and the lake became our summer playground.

Daddy built a water slide for us. We had a swing and a merry-go-round, and several row boats. In the evenings we took family boat trips. Daddy would sing and yodel. Mother who had a beautiful singing voice, sometimes sang along with him. These were happy times for us. We often built a fire on the lake shore, and sat around it watching the flames. This is when we liked to do stunts in the sand. Vern out did us girls with his backward somersaults and handsprings. Also, he could stand on his head for two whole minutes while we girls could scarcely get our heels above our head. We spent many evenings around the fire, singing and telling stories until bedtime. Ruth Knutson was our hired girl, one whom we loved and respected. She was part of our family for several years. One day a young Swede from Sweden came and wooed her away. She changed her name to Backlund, and she and Oscar moved to Minneapolis to live. Crystal and I were to see a great deal more of them in our teenage years when we, too, went to Minneapolis. We had a doll named Peggy Jane. She spent most of her time hanging upside down on the clothes line drying out after a dunking in the lake. Mother was a professional seamstress. She sewed and made all of our clothes. One summer she made us each a quilted sun hat. I remember Vern's so well, because he became very attached to it. It was made of red felt and had a little crown and a brim all the way around to shade his face and neck. He put it on in the morning for breakfast and wore it all day long. He wore it when we went swimming, and he wore it for every meal. He objected strongly to taking it off when he went to bed for the night. We had a dog named Nibs. He was a big Saint Bernard, and appointed himself bodyguard and watch dog. He guarded our line fence and our gate and was very careful whom he let in. His downfall was his over-protective attitude. We had to say good-by to him. Daddy took him away. We had many other dogs but all of them together did not compare to Nibs.

My brother Vern was about three years old at the time of this little incident that I remember so well. Crystal, Vern, and I were sent to the mail box to pick up the mail. We had a long walk down the Bushy Line Road to the mailbox. When we got there we began to quarrel over who was going to carry the mail. Vern threw his little red hat on the ground. He screamed, fell down, and passed out. Crystal and I had seen him like this before, and we knew that mother always poured water on him to bring him to. We ran to the ditch looking for water, but it was dry. We ran back to Vern, who was still lying on the ground. Something had to be done, so we puckered up our mouths and began to spit on his face. He came to at last, jumped up, put on his hat, and we all went home. We told mother the story and declared to her that we had saved his life.

Ruth saved Vern's life on one occasion when he fell into the scrub-bucket and would have drowned if she had not been there. Mother was working in the garden and Ruth had been scrubbing the floor. She left the room for a minute, and Crystal, Vern, and I all began running around the pail. Suddenly Vern lost his balance and fell in head first. Crystal and I thought he looked very funny with his feet kicking in the air. We were laughing and shouting, "Look at Vern! Look what Vern's doing." Ruth came running to see what was going on. She pulled him out of the water, choking, wet and dripping. How fortunate for Vern that we had Ruth who was always watching over us.

I retained some of my naughty ways and was sometimes a worry to my mother. How well I remember the time she was called to the home of a neighbor to help with an illness. She left Crystal, Vern, and I at home alone. As soon as she was out of our sight, we began to feel lonesome. I was determined to do something about it. I put Vern in the wagon and Crystal and I walked to the neighbors pulling the wagon. When we arrived there, mother came out to the road to meet us. "I thought I told you to stay home," she said. I spoke up knowing just the right words to say. "Well, you see, mother, we were getting so lonesome for you, we just had to come." We were allowed to stay for the rest of the day. I was lonesome for my mother whenever she got out of my sight.

On another occasion, mother drove the team and wagon to Knutson's to help Mrs. Knutson with the corn canning. Ruth Knutson was left at home to take care of us. As soon as mother left the yard, I sneaked out of the house and followed her. I stayed well back behind her and was careful that she didn't see me. I walked a long ways, and at last I turned up unannounced at Knutson's door. This hit my mother like a bomb shell. I was sent home and duly punished. In the meantime, Ruth was hunting for me, and was terrified with the thought that I had drowned in the lake or fallen into the well.

My mother was a strict disciplinarian, and was particular about our scruples. She kept a bar of yellow Fels Naptha soap and a tooth brush handy for washing out mouths. And, of course, she didn't expect us to steal as I did on one occasion. It came about like this. One day my mother took us in the horse-drawn buggy for a visit with the Knutson family. We children all played in the sand box where I discovered new and interesting treasures. I found a pretty piece of broken glass, the remains of a broken dish. I cherished it, and put it in my pocket. On the way home I took the broken glass out of my pocket and showed it to Crystal. My mother's ever watchful eye saw the treasure, too. "Where did you get that?" she asked. "Out of the sandbox," I replied. Without a word my mother turned the team around and drove back to the Knutsons. I was made to go into the house and return the glass. I had to tell them I was sorry and they couldn't doubt it, for the tears were flowing down my cheeks. I was truly impressed and remember it well to this day. The Bible says, "Thou shalt not steal." I learned a valuable lesson.

In the year of nineteen twenty the Nineteenth Amendment was passed, giving women the right to vote. I was four years old at this time. My mother was very proud of this privilege. She was determined not to neglect this duty. On that cold November morning, she hitched the team to the sled. Crystal, Vern, and I were bundled up warm and set down in a bed of hay. Mother sat up proud and tall in the front seat. She drove the horses the five long miles to the polling place.

How well I remember the excitement of those trips. We arrived at the appointed place and watched mother fill out her ballot. We children stood around the stove and warmed our hands and feet. Mother folded her ballot carefully and dropped it into a cardboard slot. Later these ballots were taken out and counted and recorded. After a short visit and a hot drink, we were ready to leave. We drove home feeling satisfied about the day. I could sense a feeling of freedom for my species. To this day I am particular that I do not abuse this great privilege.

How well I remember the Old Indian Trail that ran through our property. This trail circled Red Lake. It was used by the Indians for years before they were put onto reservations. In July the blueberries ripened and were ready for picking. This was the time for the Red Lake Indians to re-settle in the blueberry patch. These were old fashioned Indians. They traveled by horse and wagon and followed the old trail of their ancestors. How well I remember the colorful pageant they presented to us as they rode through our yard. Bucks on the wagon seats, sitting straight and tall, beating the horses and shouting in Chippewa. Squaws in colorful shawls seated in the wagon bed, cuddling their papooses in their arms. Children running and shouting, dogs barking and fighting. Young boys racing their ponies. This was a noisy and colorful scene. Our gate was their first obstacle, for my mother said they did not know how to open gates. "Run," she said, "and unfasten the gate." So we ran, and watched in wonderment as they passed by. When the blueberry season was over they took their homeward journey across our yard again. Again we ran to open the gate for them.

The Indians were treated unfairly. We saw their sufferings and were sorry.

GRANDMOTHER'S STORIES

During the winter they crowded together into poorly heated cabins and were cold and hungry. The summers were happier times. Berries and fish became plentiful. They did not plant gardens and store food for winter as we did. The Catholics built a large boarding school on the reservation town of Red Lake. Each fall they gathered up the children of school age and took them to school. They fed and clothed and educated them until spring.

I was seven years old when my daddy turned our lake shore property into a summer resort. We called our resort Ogema Beach. It was here that friends and neighbors came for Sunday outings. They went swimming and boating and ate their picnic lunches under the big elm trees. The piano in our living room got a workout as mother played the old hymns and mothers and children gathered around to sing. Daddy also built us a new frame house that summer and an outdoor dance pavilion. It was this summer that we held our first Fourth of July celebration. For this celebration we made all of our cakes, sandwiches, potato chips, and ice cream which we sold at the stands. These stands were decorated with red, white, and blue bunting. Daddy had many hired hands to do the building and to help mother in the kitchen. Hulda Olson was a big, strong Norwegian girl who kneeded the bread and beat the batter for the cakes. Evelyn Strand was a small slip of a girl who made the potato chips and washed the dishes. Elsie was born June twenty-sixth of 1922, and was one year old that summer. Mother was not well or strong. Crystal, Vern, and I watched and played, running from place to place. We were still too young to be of any help.

On the morning of the Fourth of July we got up early to be dressed and ready for the big day. Many people came from long distances and some stayed many days. Aunt Jenny, Daddy's sister, and Jane came on the train from Minneapolis. Aunt Jenny brought a hammock and hung it up between two trees in the yard and spent her time swinging and fanning and swinging, keeping cool. Mother's relatives came from Wadena and Norden. Friends and neighbors came with horse and buggy, bringing their picnic dinners and tying their horses under the trees in grassy spots to eat.

The dance band came from Kelliher to play for the evening of dancing. There was much to see, and Crystal, Vern, and I were everywhere, not missing a thing. My mother and daddy led out the first dance of the evening, dancing a beautiful waltz together. After a few minutes other couples joined them and soon the floor was crowded with dancers. After the waltz a polka was called. This is a fast-hopping dance done in couples with much swinging and twirling. When it is ended all are out of breath and gasping for air, laughing and clapping.

I remember watching my mother dress for the evening. I went into her room and found her already dressed in a long, wine-colored velvet gown which she had made for the occasion. The lamp was lit and a curling iron was heating in the chimney. Mother was brushing her long, red-brown hair, and I watched it glisten in the lamplight. After the brushing, her hair was braided and twisted into a figure eight. With a comb she ratted two locks of hair and made puffs over each ear. With the hot curling iron she curled a few loose bangs over her forehead. Mother had soft, blue-violet eyes, and she looked down and smiled at me. I remember thinking that she had to be the most beautiful woman in the world. Crystal and I were dressed in our best for the evening, and walked with my mother to the dance. We sat on the built-in benches around the dance floor, and watched the crowd of young girls doing the Charleston, a kind of lively dance done in four-four time. Their feet twisted, their heels flew and short skirts bounced. I watched and learned. Soon my handsome, Irish daddy came and asked us to dance. He danced one dance with each of us. He bought us an ice cream cone, kissed us good-night, and sent us to the house and to bed. Our big eventful day was over.

John Halvorson, transportation in winter in Northern Minnesota.

Friends and neighbors, unknown, 1915.

Our home on Red Lake built about 1923. Picture taken in 1983.

The beautiful shore of Red Lake on Ogema Beach. Picture taken in 1983.

GRANDMOTHER'S STORIES

CRIME ON RED LAKE

We had crime in our day too. How well I remember the trouble our family was involved in.

Daddy had hired help to build our house and pavalion. Protano, a short, stocky Italian was known to be the best carpenter around. Daddy hired him to be our head carpenter for the summer project. Protano was not with us very long before we realized we had a serious problem. His temper was short and fierce. He carried a gun under his shirt and he told my daddy that he and his brother were enemies, and when they met they would shoot each other on sight. Protano was a killer, and before this story is over he will have shot and killed five people. My personal interest in this story is that my daddy's name was on Protano's death list.

When Protano first came to work for us he showed great interest in the lake. He would look across the lake to the north shore and into Canada, which was twenty miles beyond. He remarked at what a good place this would be to make a get-away. Protano also brought five timber wolf cubs with him, and while he was with us, one of the cubs disappeared. He was angry over this, and accused my daddy of taking it. This, we believed, put my daddy's name on the death list.

Protano was also in love with a local girl, who did not respond to his attentions. This brought on a lot of good-natured teasing by Protano's friend, Boyd. The teasing continued until Protano became desperate. One Sunday morning he took his gun and went to the girl's home. He shot her and her mother and father. Following the shooting, he went to Boyd's home. At gun point he forced Boyd to get a pencil and paper and write a list of all the people he was going to kill. Boyd was forced to put his name at the top of the list, my daddy's name was at the bottom. While Boyd was busy writing, someone knocked on the door. It was the sheriff. Boyd threw open the door and bolted out shouting, "Don't shoot me. Get Protano. He's right behind me." Protano escaped through the back window of the cabin and disappeared into the woods.

The hunt was on. The sheriff from Bemidji was called in on the chase. Old Bean was deputized to accompany him. Bean was well-known in the community. He was the owner and operator of the livery stable. The two men drove out into the country on an old gravel road. As they drove along they spotted Protano coming out of the woods. The sheriff stopped the car, got out, and walked up to him. Protano shot him through the head. Bean was out of the car by this time, and Protano aimed two shots at his head. Bean ducked and rolled into the ditch. He crawled on his belly in the ditch for two-and-a-half miles. On reaching town he ran home. As he entered the kitchen, his wife noticed a hole in his hat. The hat became a signet of courage for the community. It hung for many years on a wooden peg in Bean's Livery Barn.

Another sheriff walked alone through the woods. He came upon a cabin half hidden in the underbrush. "This is it," he thought. "This is where I get my man." He pulled out his revolver, kicked open the door and stepped in. A bootlegger, sitting by his still in a corner of the room leaped for cover. The amazed sheriff collapsed in a chair. The bootlegger recovered first and extended his hospitality. "Sheriff, you could use a drink, and I have here just what you need." "Don't mind if I do," the sheriff answered with a longing look at the still. The sheriff and the moonshiner sat down together, each with a bracing drink of bootlegger's whiskey.

In the meantime, our family was at home making plans for Protano's visit to us. My daddy said that when Protano came to borrow a boat to make his get-a-way into Canada, he wasn't going to get it. There was going to be a shoot-out. Daddy and mother talked over their plans, and we watched in terror as they practiced their strategy. When Protano knocked on the door, my mother was to pick up the lamp and open the door, shining the light in his face. My daddy was to stand behind mother with the gun and do the shooting over her shoulder. But daddy found that he had only one shell left in his 30-30. He hurried to Rogers store to buy more shells. Due to the crisis in the community the store was out of ammunition. They could find only one shell for my daddy's 30-30. He came home with the sad report that he would have only two shells with which to face Protano. We lived in fear for several days. In the evening we pinned newspapers over the windows and turned the lights down low. We sat in fear waiting for the dreaded knock on the door. Finally the news came that Protano was taken into custody, but not until he had killed another sheriff, making five deaths in all. Protano was sentenced to life in the penitentiary. People from our community visited him, and reports came back that he became an old man overnight. His hair had turned white. He was eighty years old when he was offered his freedom. He was unhappy with the outside world and returned to the penitentiary. They gave him an unlocked cell, and there he lived until he died.

My dear children, crime does not pay. The Bible says, "Thou shalt not kill." God's laws give us explicit guidelines for living. I knew little of them in those days.

GRANDMOTHER'S STORIES

Kelliher Reunion; Crystal Murphy, Buel Maynard, Wanda Stenberg, and Laura Halvorson.

Kelliher Jubilee and Reunion; Grace Clemenson, Buel Maynard, Maggie Maynard, Laura Halverson, Wanda Stenberg, Crystal Murphy, Maurice Stenberg, Kathleen Murphy, 1983.

Our neighbors on Red Lake; Jens and Johanna Sophia Knudsen, wedding picture.

GRANDMOTHER'S STORIES

OUR NEIGHBORS ON RED LAKE

Grones were our nearest and dearest neighbors. We saw them often. Mrs. Grone was a small, stout woman with a big smile and sunny disposition. Mother, Crystal, Vern, Elsie and I walked to their little log cabin home on many a sunny afternoon. How well I remember the dough gobs Mrs. Grone served to us hot from the kettle, all sprinkled with cinnamon and sugar. I remember, too, the many times Mrs. Grone, Helen, Myrtle and baby came to see us. We children played in the sand by the lake while the mothers talked and laughed, reviewing the neighborhood gossip. Coffee brewed on the stove and cinnamon rolls baked in the oven.

The Urseths lived across the road from the Grones. Mrs. Urseth loved flowers and grew them abundantly. Her big front yard was a massive flower garden in the summertime. I imagined myself in fairy land as I walked down the path to her front door with the golden-glow waving over my head. Mrs. Urseth had a talent for making paper flowers. How well I remember the colorful bouquet she made for Grandpa Johnston's casket. She was a generous and warm-hearted person.

The Nyrene's lived around the lake from us to the east. They were of Swedish descent, and lived in the Swedish community, while we, being of Scotch and Irish descent, lived in the Norwegian community. The Nyrenes owned lakeshore property. The annual summer neighborhood picnic was held on their big, grassy lawn facing the lake. The 4th of July picnic was sometimes held there, too, complete with an outdoor podium decorated in red, white, and blue bunting. Benches were placed under the trees, and here the parents sat listening to political speeches. Men running for county office or any one who had an ax to grind could grind it at the 4th of July picnic. How we children looked forward to these get-togethers. Happily we walked down the dusty road, carrying our picnic baskets.

How well I remember the Sunday dinners we enjoyed in the Nyrene's home during the long, cold winter months. Mother would hitch up our faithful horse, Tommy, to the sleigh and away we'd all go with the snow flying around us. Tommy was always in a hurry when he knew there was a warm barn ahead. What fun we had playing with our friend, Mable, who was our age. We played in the haymow and in the snow, rolling over and over and sinking deep in the soft fluff.

The Rogers lived around the lake to the west. Mrs. Rogers was a big, jolly heavy set woman who was always glad to see us and greeted us with bear hugs. Mary Rogers was the only daughter. She was two years older than I. We complained about her sometimes. We thought she was bossy. She was popular with us though, because she kept kittens. She had a pretty little basket with a little mattress and doll blankets, and tucked inside were three or four baby kittens. When we went there we were allowed to play with them under Mary's close supervision. We could put them in the doll buggy and push them around or wrap them in a blanket and rock them to sleep. When one brood grew too big for the basket, there was always a new litter to take its place. Mary was seldom without baby kittens.

We went to the Rogers often, walking barefoot in the warm sand along the lake shore. Sometimes Mother got out the boat and we rowed from our beach to their beach, a distance of three miles. In the wintertime we walked the mile and a half through the woods on the old Indian trail. One cold day in early November our family rode over to Rogers' store in the sleigh. While we were in Mrs. Rogers' kitchen warming our hands over her big cook stove we saw a flock of geese flying over the lake. Daddy quickly grabbed his gun and ran out shooting. As we watched, one big goose came falling through the sky down into the lake. The Rogers boys, George and Thornton, jumped into the boat and rowed out to pick it up. They plucked it and cleaned it. Mrs. Rogers said we would all be staying for dinner. Mother peeled potatoes, Mrs. Rogers stuffed the goose. They put squash in the oven. Mary set the table. George and Thornton got out the ice cream freezer and ice from the ice house. In no time at all we had a wild goose dinner with home-made ice cream. We stayed there all day, and what an exciting day it was!

The Rogers owned and operated the Shotley Brook Store. They also built a big hotel on the lakeshore which accommodated the lumberjacks, sailors, and early settlers. Our family stayed there several weeks while daddy was getting our log cabin home ready for us on Ogema Beach. We bought most of our groceries at the Shotley Brook store. In the summers we did our shopping by row boat, rowing to the store, loading our boat, and rowing home.

The Knutsens, too, were some of my mother's favorite people. We exchanged visits with them, going back and forth for picnics and corn canning bees. How well I remember the corn canning days. We all got up early and went to the field to pick the corn and haul it in. Our white gelding, Tommy, helped us by pulling the loaded dray. We piled the corn on the picnic table in the front yard. Daddy sharpened the knives, mother got out the pans for the cutting. Ruth, our hired girl, had the breakfast ready of pancakes and syrup. Soon the Knutson family arrived—a whole wagon load of them. Everyone was given a job to do. We children began the husking and silking. Water had to be pumped and carried for the boilers. Wood was cut and brought in to keep the fires going. Jars were scrubbed and cleaned. Mother and Mrs. Knutson cut the corn off the cob and packed it into jars. The rubbers and lids were put on and the jars were put into the copper boilers on the stove. There they were boiled for three hours. While these were cooking we set the table for a big picnic, which included all the corn we could eat. Ruth was a good hand at baking, and brought out two pans of gingerbread and set them on the table to finish up on. Lunch over, we were back in the field, picking more corn. More jars were washed and packed and sealed. When the first batch came off the second batch was ready to go on. This was an all-day job, and no play day for us. We all had work to do and how we enjoyed the day!

Our Shotley neighbors, Mrs. Crone, Mr. and Mrs. Nyrene, 1951.

GRACE CLEMENSON

The Shotley Brook School.

Shotley Brook School children, teacher, Miss Daily at far left, Crystal and Grace Johnston in nickers.

GRANDMOTHER'S STORIES

SCHOOL DAYS AT THE SHOTLEY BROOK SCHOOL

In the fall of 1923, Crystal and I started school. Crystal was six years old and I was seven. Mother started us together so we could be company and a help for each other on those long, two mile walks. The weather was fierce, stormy, and bitterly cold in winter on the Canadian border.

Mother sewed warm clothes for us. Our coats, caps, leggings, and mittens were all homemade. How well I remember the big black velvet muffs mother made for us, and the beaver fur hat she made for me. We did keep warm, and with our lunch pails over our arms and our hands in our muffs we trudged along. When we came to the Bushy Line corner, we joined other children and all walked together.

The Nyrenes lived several miles from school, and Julien had a horse and sleigh to drive, changing to a buggy in the fall and spring. His sisters, Mable and Esther, rode with him. Julien would often stop and call off the name of a child to ride with him. He also kept an eye on the younger ones who might be getting cold. Crystal and I both would get our turn to ride, and what a joy to go racing away, the horse at a gallop and the snow flying around us. At school there was a warm barn for the horse and hay in the manger.

The Shotley Brook School was a one-room school, large and spacious. A large porch decorated the whole front of the building. Two doors opening off the porch and into the school led us into our cloak rooms. In the girls' cloak room were hooks along the wall, and here we hung our coats and stacked our lunch pails underneath. In the wintertime our lunch pails were set around the stove to keep our food from freezing. Our desks were in rows, one row for each grade. The teacher's big desk stood in front of the room and at the back of the room stood a huge black wood-burning heater. Blackboards lined three walls and six big windows filled the west wall. On the front wall over the teacher's desk hung the big school clock. Beside the clock hung a picture of Abraham Lincoln.

Our school had a library. Two walls from ceiling to floor were filled with books. Long, large windows on the south wall gave ample light for reading. We had no electric lights in those days. Little tables and chairs were placed invitingly around the room. I always felt a great delight, when I finished my assignments and received permission, to go to the library. I browsed through the book shelves and chose a book to read. How well I remember *Mrs. Wiggs of the Cabbage Patch* and her large brood of unruly children, *The Belgium Twins* and their struggle through World War I, *The Irish Twins* carried me away to a fairy land of shady glens and leprechauns. With *The Dutch Twins* I visited the dykes and watched the big arms of the windmills swinging around in the breeze. I went with them as they delivered milk by dog cart and ate little frosted cakes which were purchased from the street vendors. The beautiful countryside and quaint life styles held me spell-bound.

Our drinking fountain was a large crock cooler with a spigot at the bottom. Each child brought his own drinking cup from home and kept it in his desk. When we wanted a drink we would raise our hand for permission to go to the fountain. We children were assigned work around the school and oftentimes it would be my job to fill the water crock from the well outside. I had a pail I set under the pump and after pumping the handle for a long time, I filled the pail with water and carried it to the fountain. This wasn't my favorite job. I had to do it at recess or at noon and it took away a little of my play time.

There were six of us in the first grade that fall of 1923—Mable Nyrene, Hollis Grone, Leonard Anderson, Harry Munson, and Crystal and I. By the beginning of our third year, two were missing. Harry Munson was killed when a tree his father was cutting down fell on him. It was summertime, and a neighbor boy ran from home to home to give us the sad news. Harry was running and would have escaped the tree, but his father, intending to help him, grabbed his shirt tail and pulled him back under the path of the falling tree. We were all saddened by this event, and were doubly sorry for the father. It was said that he never did forgive himself or fully recover from the shock. Hollis Grone died of quinsy during one of our long, hard winters. Hollis had been a faithful member of the summer Bible School. He had a firm faith in Jesus. It was said that as he was dying, he sat up in bed, raised up his arms and cried, "Oh, Jesus, take me." So he went with Jesus, and his family was comforted with the thought at seeing him again on resurrection morning.

Miss Daily was our firey little Irish teacher. She was small in build, but made up for it in determination. She had Irish blue eyes, black curly hair, and a ruddy complexion. She had a quick temper and was a firm disciplinarian. She kept us all in line. We never moved from our seats without first raising our hand for permission. If we wanted a drink of water, we raised our hand. If our pencil needed sharpening, we raised our hand. If we needed to go to the outhouse, we raised our hand. Miss Daily's kindness and sense of humor won our hearts. I can still see her laughing at our little jokes. We all loved her. She loved all of us.

One of the first things Miss Daily did when she took over our school was to hang up a demerit chart. Anyone having an over-abundance of demerits was not allowed to take part in the special Friday afternoon activities. Friday afternoons were full of surprises. First we had a meeting of the Little Citizens' Club. We elected officers, discussed problems, and voted on punishments to fit the crimes. After the meeting we had arts and crafts, or a singspiration, or a party. Sometimes Miss Daily would read to us from a favorite book.

I remember so well at one of our meetings of the Little Citizens' Club when my name came up for the discussion of a misdemeanor. I do not remember my crime, but it was voted and seconded that I would be required to wash all six of the big windows in the main room. I was to stay in for recess and noon hour until the job was finished. This was to take me probably a full week. This was by all counts a severe punishment. When my mother heard of it, she protested very strongly. She thought the punishment far exceeded the crime. She came to school and talked with Juliene, our Little Citizens' president, and with Miss Daily. So it was voted upon again at the next meeting and decided that I should wash just two of the windows. The remaining four were to wait for another culprit.

Spelling was one of my difficult subjects. I was probably a third grader and seldom if ever got a perfect score on a spelling test. So when on one occasion I got a grade of one hundred I was elated. I took the paper home to show my parents. My mother looked at it and smiled, but when she turned the paper over and saw all the words written out on the underside of the sheet, she frowned and looked unhappy. My daddy took a sterner view, and said he knew that I had cheated. He said that Santa Claus does not bring gifts to children who cheat, and that I would get no gifts that year. He spanked me and sent me to bed without any supper. I cried bitterly. My mother came to my room to talk to me. I was a firm believer in Santa Claus, and He was my main concern. I told my mother that I would get gifts in my stocking on Christmas Eve. Santa Claus knows everything about me, and he knows that I didn't cheat. Mother looked sad and sympathetic, as she quickly left the room. Soon daddy came to talk to me and apologized. He took me to the kitchen for a late supper.

Mother and Miss Daily became close friends. Mother worked closely with her on school programs and projects. Mother served as clerk on the school board, and together Miss Daily and mother chose the books for the school library. Mother played the organ for the school programs. How well I remember the Wand Drill we put on for one of our Christmas programs. The costumes were made of white crepepaper, we wore white skirts and tops, with large paper wings trimmed with gold-colored tinsel. The crowns were white with gold tinsel and wands were made of dowels covered with white crepepaper with a gold star on the tip. For several weeks we practiced our march and our drills. On opening night we all crowded into the library to dress. We took off our shoes and pulled on long white stockings. We put on our white dresses, our wings, and our crowns. We took our wands in our hands and waited for mother to strike the opening chord on the organ, — our signal to march out. Miss Daily opened the door and out we came, paper skirts rustling. No matter that the crowns got a little tipsy and the wings a little bent. We were angels with magic wands and crowns of gold. We marched in formation and swung our wands, keeping time to the music. Back in the library we heard the house coming down with loud clapping and laughter. Miss Daily opened the library door and beckoned us back to the stage. Mother played another march and we smiled and waved our wands. The parents were delighted.

Smallpox was a dreaded and deadly disease, characterized by high fever and skin blisters, a disease that left you scarred with pox marks. A serum had been discovered to eradicate it. The state of Minnesota passed a law that all school children must be vaccinated. Miss Daily received a notice to prepare the children and to have everyone present at the school house on a certain date. Vaccination was a strange new word in our community. Smallpox was so frightening that the idea of injecting the germ into the body could not be understood by some parents. We were not given the freedom of choice. This was a law and we must obey it. As far as I know we all did. Mother and Miss Daily approved the plan, but some parents did not and were angry and frightened.

The day arrived and how well I remember the dread that hung over our school. Parents came bringing their children. Doctor Bone was there with his little black satchel. He opened it up on the teacher's desk and laid out the cotton, alcohol, bandages, and needles. He told us that he would put three scratches on our left arm. We rolled up our sleeves and stood in line. Some children were crying, one fainted. We all were looking a little pale. Mother and Miss Daily helped the doctor and comforted the children. When my turn came I stepped up to the desk. I looked at the needle and quaked with fright, expecting some great stab of pain. I looked at my mother and she smiled at me. To my surprise there was no pain at all. The cool alcohol numbed my skin and the three little scratches were hardly felt. Mother put on the sterile pad and bandage. I rolled down my sleeve and wondered what the fuss was all about. I must admit I was slightly disappointed and felt let down to think that it was done so quickly and easily.

The real test came later, when at home that evening we all began to get sick. Our arms became red and swollen, and quite painful. Heads ached and stomachs churned. We were sick with a light form of smallpox. School was closed for several days. The fear of death by smallpox was gone forever.

GRANDMOTHER'S STORIES

North Dakota relatives; Otis Tye, Lizzie Tye and Ruby Tye with Champ Maynard, July 1941.

Johnston Sisters; Crystal, Grace and Elsie, about 1939.

Mary Johnston and daughter Elsie.

Vern Maynard Johnston, Grove Lake, Minnesota, 1932.

GRANDMOTHER'S STORIES

FUNKLEY

The little farms in the north woods were largely self-supporting. We had a Jersey cow for milk, cream and butter. We had a few chickens for eggs. We kept a few sheep for their wool to sell on the market. Mother also carded wool and made warm wool quilts. We sometimes had a pig. Mother always raised a big garden. We picked wild raspberries and blueberries for sauce. We picked wild plums and high bush cranberries for jelly and syrup. Mother canned fish and venison. She would sometimes have as much as a thousand quarts of fruit and vegetables stored for winter. Still, my daddy was gone a lot, working out wherever he could find work. We needed money for thread and needles, for boots and shoes, for staple goods and oil for our lamps.

We lived here on the shore of Red Lake until I was ten years old and in the fourth grade. In November of that year we moved to Funkley. Funkley was a lumberjack and railroad town, with a rough and tough reputation. The population was about two hundred. We moved there in November of 1926. We lived in a little two room shack by the side of the railroad track. Big steam locomotives steamed by day and night, rattling and shaking our little house. We had lost our home on Ogema Beach. My daddy had failed to keep up the payments. He rented this little farm near Funkley and moved us there.

The Funkley school was the center of the social activities. The school functions were held here as well as the neighborhood dances. It was a very rustic looking building, tall and bleak with white paint peeling. A little step at the front entrance lead into one main cloak hall. A wood shed was attached to the back. Two outhouses stood in the back yard. This school offered no frills. How well I remember my disappointment and unbelief. The drinking fountain was a water pail with a common drinking dipper. An old fashioned bookcase with broken glass doors served as our library. A big wood burning heater stood at the back of the room and behind it was a door leading to the woodshed. The older boys were excused to cut wood and the sound of chopping was often heard during classes. The woodshed, too, served another function. It was a correction center for unruly boys who were taken there for their strappings.

There was a great deal of fighting going on among the boys. I learned to hold my own when we were stopped on the way home from school for a gang fight. It was Vern and I against the town roughnecks. On one occasion they surrounded my brother and had him down. I ran to him and started hitting. One boy swung his lunch pail and hit me on the cheek bone. I carried the scar for years. My father came to our rescue. He was very angry and went to talk with the parents. He told them that the fighting would be done by the fathers. He challenged them one by one to come out and fight him. They all backed off. This put an end to the gang fighting.

Our religious training was rather scanty, though I know now the Holy Spirit was at work. My mother was raised a Methodist. She had a Bible packed away in a trunk. I remember seeing it only once, when on a Sunday morning she took it out to read to us. Mother learned to play the organ when she was a young girl. Now we had a piano in our home and mother loved to play. We listened to the old Methodist hymns which mother played and sang for us. My daddy was brought up in the Presbyterian faith. It was from him that I first heard the children's song, "Jesus Loves Me." He sang it over and over until I learned it. We were taught to say a little prayer at night, the old familiar "Now I Lay Me Down to Sleep." This was the extent of our early religious training. It was at Funkley that I became better acquainted with Jesus and I gave my heart to Him. A very devout Lutheran family lived on a farm near us. They held Wednesday night prayer meetings in their home. My mother and I attended several of these meetings. How well I remember kneeling by my chair and listening to the prayers. On Sunday mornings the Hanson family went into town and opened up the town hall for Sunday school. Mother and we children were attracted to this and often walked into town on Sunday mornings. It was here that I learned my first Bible verse, John 3:16. "For God so loved the world that He gave his only begotten Son that whosoever believeth in Him shall not perish but have everlasting life." In the summertime, tent meetings were held in the nearby town of Blackduck. A group of Lutheran young people from the Lutheran College came to conduct these meetings. These were old fashioned revival meetings held in a big tent with a sawdust floor. We sat on wooden benches arranged in front of a platform. On the platform was a piano and a pulpit. Here the song leader led out with the old revival songs. The old tent rocked as we sang "Power in the Blood" and "Revive Us Again." Here I was converted. We were given little New Testament Bibles and were told we should read them every day and pray. This little Bible was my special treasure and went with me on all of my teenage journeys. I formed the habit of reading a Scripture and saying my prayers before bedtime.

I was my daddy's right hand man, helping him with the outdoor work around the farm. My mother often said he couldn't move without me. I worked with him in the garden riding Betsy on the cultivator, cultivating corn and potatoes. I milked cows, I pitched hay and made stacks. One warm summer afternoon Vern and I, daddy and Uncle Buel, were making hay in a little meadow near our home. We rode into the hayfield in a big hay wagon pulled by our two horses, Betsy and

GRANDMOTHER'S STORIES

Topsy. When we reached the meadow we unhitched the horses and let them graze while we did some hand raking. Suddenly from the woods behind me I heard the call of a wolf. One long, anxious, excited call. Then in the distance I heard an answering call, and soon several wolves were barking and talking. They gathered into a pack, ran out into the field and began to rush us. Daddy and Uncle Buel ran for the horses. They quickly hitched them to the wagon and called to Vern and me to jump in. It was all done so quickly and as daddy whipped the horses, we galloped away. The wolves followed a short distance and gave up the chase. Daddy said they were after the horses. Daddy and Uncle Buel went back with their guns, but could find no trace of the wolves. Like silent ghosts, they faded into the wilderness.

We lost our beloved Tommy soon after we moved to Funkley. Tommy was a beautiful white gelding, full of life and full of speed. Daddy bought him at a horse sale while we were still living at Shotley. He took us on many fast sled rides and performed small chores around the farm. One of our cows, the leader of the herd, had a grudge against Tommy. She had a full set of wicked-looking horns and several times we saw her making threatening stabs at him. Mother reminded daddy many times to have her dehorned. The chore was put off too long. One evening we returned home from an all day outing and found Tommy lying in the pasture, dead. His stomach had been ripped open and we knew exactly who the culprit was. The next day daddy dehorned the cow and we buried Tommy with many tears. We never again owned a horse like him, and we never again loved a horse as we did Tommy.

Daddy was of Scotch and Irish descent. He was raised in a Scottish community in Iowa. There he wore Scottish kilts as a boy and learned to dance the Highland Fling. I was about twelve years old when I coaxed my daddy into teaching me to dance. While mother and Crystal sang, I waved my arms and tapped my toes to the tune of *Turkey in the Straw*. I learned several steps and we spent many happy evenings singing and clapping while I danced. How well I remember the time my mother and I took the train to Gonvick to visit Uncle John and Aunt Laura and all the cousins. One Saturday night I was told that we would be going to a house party at Uncle Willy's and I would be asked to dance the Highland Fling. While Uncle Willie played *Turkey in the Straw* on his accordian, I danced through all my steps. Soon I heard everyone clapping and I saw pennies, nickles, and dimes sliding across the floor. When the dance was over, I picked up three dollars and eighty cents in change. I was breathless and excited. Mother and I went to Bemidji to choose a lasting gift to commemorate the occasion. A picture called *The Lone Wolf* pictured a wolf standing alone on a snow covered hill, calling to his mate on a cold winter night, hung for some time in our living room.

GRACE CLEMENSON

In May of 1930 I graduated from the eighth grade. How well I remember the pretty black and white check dress with the red trim that mother made for me for this event. Our teacher, Miss Parent, planned a last day of school program. As the program ended, Miss Parent called our attention to a special announcement. Grace Johnston had been selected by a student vote to receive the outstanding citizenship award given by The American Legion. This award was designated to the abilities, of courage, character, service, companionship and scholarship. This came as a complete surprise to me. I was called to the front of the room to receive my award. There were smiles all around and much clapping. I was praised and congratulated and realized that I was loved and accepted in this community. It was a happy day for me.

I celebrated my fifteenth birthday on July the third. I was beginning to feel quite grown up. Mother, Crystal and I were making plans for the time when Crystal and I would go away to school. There were no high schools in our community. The stockmarket crash of 1929 brought a chill into our home. When we lived at Shotley, we felt secure and comfortable. Our move to Funkley ended in the break-up of our home. Jobs were scarce during the Great Depression. Daddy could no longer pick up the odd jobs needed to keep the flour in the flour bin and shoes on our feet. He became discouraged and left us.

In the summer of 1930 mother and we children stayed home. Though food was scarce, we had a garden and some chickens and a cow. I remember working in a hotel for several weeks and with this money I bought some of the staple groceries needed. Mother kept busy sewing school clothes for Crystal and me. How well I remember the plaid jackets and matching tams she made for each of us. All too soon summer was over, the last time we would all be home together. We all said goodbye. Vern, who was thirteen, went to live with a neighbor on a nearby farm. Crystal and I took the train to Minneapolis. From there I went into Faribolt to the State School for the Deaf.

Mother and Elsie were left home alone, but not for long. Mother suffered a gall bladder attack and went to the University Hospital for an operation. Mother's convalescent period was spent with her Uncle Jack and Aunt Esther at their farm home in Grove Lake. In the spring of 1931 mother went back to Funkley to get her household belongings. The house had been ransacked and everything was gone. Mother had lost her husband, three of her children, and her worldly belongings. She went back to Grove Lake where she took a housekeeping job for an elderly man who was a close friend of her father.

GRANDMOTHER'S STORIES

Vern, Grace, Crystal, Elsie Johnston, about 1930, Funkley, Minnesota.

Elsie Johnston, Summer, 1932.

Vern Johnston, 1933.

Mary Johnston

George Otis Johnston, 1936.

GRACE CLEMENSON

Elsie Johnston and Pearl Backlund, Minneapolis, Minnesota, 1937.

Crystal Johnston and Oscar Backlund Jr., Minneapolis, 1937.

GRANDMOTHER'S STORIES

SCHOOL FOR THE DEAF

Now you remember that when I was four years old I had been sick with scarlet fever. As a result of this, I had developed abscesses in both ears. I was developing a serious hearing problem. My parents made arrangements for me to attend the State School for the Deaf at Faribault, Minnesota.

I felt strangely out of place as I watched the other girls in the dormitory communicating in sign language. I was put in the lower wing of the dormitory and assigned to a room with eight beds. Each bed had a chest of drawers, a chair, and a small closet. The girls in this room were all hard-of-hearing. They spoke English as I did. Now I set out to find a special friend. A tall girl by the name of Ann Coldwell came to my rescue. Ann had been there the previous year. She had a room in the upper wing with an extra bed. Ann invited me to be her roommate. Miss Emery, the dean of girls, gave her consent. Together Ann and I carried my luggage to her room. Ann was a neat housekeeper. The beds were made up with matching spreads. A library table and two chairs stood in one corner. There were braided rugs on the floor and potted plants in the window. This was a comfortable arrangement. Ann and I remained best friends throughout the school year.

A bright spot of the school year was our formal dances. I had a boy friend, too, a tall, skinny red-head. He was my escort to all of the parties. Verner Henderson was also a favorite of my house mother, who would sometimes grant us special privileges. On one occasion we were preparing for the Valentine Sweetheart Ball. Verner was put in charge of decorations. He decided that he needed my help. However, this was my day to clear tables in the dining room. I knew there was no way I could get out of that job. Verner knew a way. He went to talk to Miss Emery. Miss Emery was a large, heavy-set woman with a firm, stern look and a heart of gold. She was in the dining room when Verner walked in. I saw them talking. I saw Miss Emery nodding her head. Miss Emery sent another girl to take over my job and I walked out with Verner. We went to the gym and spent the rest of the afternoon working on party decorations.

The dance was on Saturday night. We girls kept busy washing and curling our hair, laughing and giggling. My mother made my formal for me. I was tall and skinny and mother knew this. The dress was a perfect fit. I dressed and went to the girls' parlor to wait for my escort. Verner looked very fine in his new blue suit and tie. He nodded to me. I stood up and we walked out. We danced until midnight. Miss Emery was there smiling at us and watching over the refreshments. We ate a

GRACE CLEMENSON

sugar cookes and drank a glass of punch. The party was over. Vernor and I walked back to the girls' dormitory. We said good-night. Verner squeezed my hand and left in it a tiny box. "See you in the morning," he said. I knew he would. Verner was the tallest boy in school, and I was the tallest girl. We had the privilege of being first in line for the dining room line-up. I led the march proudly that day wearing my new sweetheart locket. The Valentine Sweetheart Ball remains a precious memory.

Grace Clemenson and friend Ann Coldwell at the school for the deaf of Faribault, Minnesota, Spring 1932.

GRANDMOTHER'S STORIES

HIGH SCHOOL DAYS IN GLENWOOD

I left the State School for the Deaf. I was unhappy there. I was not getting the education I wanted. I wanted to go to high schoool. Mother helped me to enroll in a small school in Glenwood, Minnesota. Mother and Elsie were there working on a farm. I entered the home of the Norgaard family. Mr. Norgaard was Superintendent of the Glenwood schools. I lived with them and worked for my room and board through my freshman and sophomore years. Norgaards were a lovely family. They had two children, a girl, Katherine, who was two years old and a baby whom they called Baby Brother. My duties were to be a mother's helper. This consisted of child care and babysitting, ironing clothes, washing dishes and cleaning house. Mrs. Norgaard did the washing, cooking and baking. I received no money for these services. Mother sent me postage stamps and a dollar when she could. She also sewed some of my clothes. Mrs. Norgaard bought my school supplies and personal items. Here in the year of 1932 I began my freshman year of high school. How well I remember the first day of school. How thrilled I was to be there. I was sixteen years old now. I was five feet seven and one-half inches tall and of slender build. I had red-brown hair and blue eyes and a big, friendly smile. I was known as "Norgaard's girl." I quickly gained in popularity. I was elected to play on the freshman girls basketball team. In my sophomore year I was elected to the Glenwood Girl's Honor Society. I studied hard, worked hard, and played hard.

I had several close girl friends, and we often went downtown on Saturday nights. A big attraction in the park on Saturday night was the band concert. We sat around on the park benches and ate popcorn and watched the boys play their marches. Tiring of this, we went into the stores to look and to shop. We had our girl parties on Saturday nights too. We took turns entertaining. I was always proud when my turn came. Mrs. Norgaard made cakes and cookies and set the jello. She made a pot of hot chocolate, then excused herself and left us to enjoy the evening. We quickly set up the card tables and got the cards out for a game of progressive whist. When we tired of this, we turned the radio on to the Saturday night barn dances and danced polkas and waltzes in the kitchen.

Our parties were not all girl parties. One time we were invited to a Valentine party at a girl friend's home. We were instructed to each bring a boy friend. Mrs. Norgaard told me that there was only one boy I could go out with, and that was my cousin, Guy. I wrote to Guy and invited him to the party. He came for me in his Model T Ford. The party was a great success. We played progressive whist, danced, ate, and talked. Guy described the party later to Crystal. "Grace was the most popular girl there, and of course, I was the most popular boy." Guy lived in the country near Grove Lake. Uncle Jack and Aunt Either farmed. Guy lived at home helping them on the farm. Lee, Guy's younger brother, was a seventh grader at the local grade school.

Uncle Jack's home was my second home. I went there for special long weekends and school holidays. Though I worked hard at Norgaards and studied hard at school, my vacations here were carefree and joyous. I rode to town with Uncle Jack in his horse drawn buggy. We sold eggs and bought groceries. I went with Guy visiting friends and neighbors. Crystal came for Christmas one year. We skated on the lake those cold winter evenings, warming our hands over a brush fire and drinking hot chocolate. Evenings we cranked up the old Victrola and danced to the tune of *"My Sweet Little Alice Blue Gown"* and *"Sidewalks of New York."* How well I remember the time that Lee and I were doing a polka. Faster and faster we went until Lee caught his toe in a crack on the floor and went down, pulling me down on top of him. We lay there laughing. Crystal and Guy were laughing too. Uncle Jack didn't think it was so funny. He was trying to sleep. He came storming out. He growled and complained. We played the record over and Lee and I finished our polka. Finally Uncle Jack persuaded us to go to bed. Good night, *Sweet Alice Blue Gown.*

In the spring of my sophomore year, May of 1934, Aunt Either died. She had suffered four years from breast cancer. Her sister, my grandmother Minnie, had also died of breast cancer. How well I remember the day Uncle Jack brought Aunt Either home from the doctor's office. The doctor had said that her end was near and had sent her home to die. It was Easter vacation and Crystal and I were visiting there. Guy and Lee were home and we were all standing in the kitchen when they came in. Aunt Either was thin and weak and her breathing was coming in short gasps. Uncle Jack carried her to a chair. She felt more comfortable sitting up than lying down. Tears came to Uncle Jack's eyes as he said to the boys, "This was your mother's last trip to the doctor." We knew what he meant. We were sober and saddened.

When Aunt Either and I were alone together, we often read from the Bible. I usually read out loud to her. Now she wanted me to read again. We went into the living room and sat down together as we had done many times before. I opened the Bible to John fourteen and read verses one through five. "In my Father's house are many mansions. If it were not so I would have told you. I go to prepare a place for you, and if I go I will come again and receive you unto Myself, that where I am there ye may be also." Then I turned to the twenty-third psalm. Before I had finished, Aunt Either had fallen asleep in her chair.

GRANDMOTHER'S STORIES

Aunt Either lived another six weeks. It was in May just before Memorial Day that a friend of Guy's came for me. "Your aunt is dying and she is asking for you," he said. I hurried to her bedside. She was propped up on pillows and was repeating the words "read, read, read." A neighbor woman was there reading to her from a magazine. I knew what she really wanted. She wanted her Bible. At that minute, as I stood at the foot of her bed she took her last breath and sank back on the pillows. Uncle Jack was leaning over her and crying out her name over and over. "Either, Either," he cried. Aunt Either, as if in response, raised up on the pillow, opened her eyes and looked at him. Then with a last, long sigh she was gone out of our reach forever. I tried in my awkward way to comfort him. There was no comfort — only pain. Mother and Elsie arrived the next day. It was a comfort to see them. We were comforted, too, by many friends.

The undertakers came to the home to prepare the body. A casket was brought in. She looked beautiful lying there. Aunt Either was a beautiful woman, tall and slender with black hair and large brown eyes. The most beautiful of all was her wide friendly smile.

Now she will sleep until Jesus comes. I know I will see her again. We will sit together at Jesus' feet and listen to Him read from His Word; the words she loved to hear.

Grovelake Church and Cemetery taken in 1947.

Elsie Johnston with Mother Mary Johnston and Georgie Johnston.

Guy Hart, about 1934.

Elsie Johnston and Vern Johnston, hauling hay.

GRANDMOTHER'S STORIES

JEWISH FAMILY

School was out for the summer. I had finished my sophomore year at Glenwood. I decided to go to Minneapolis and join Crystal who was working there. We had been separated for two years, only seeing each other on occasion. During the summer Crystal and I worked and lived next door to each other. We lived on the north side of Minneapolis in Jewish homes. This was an interesting summer. I was seventeen years old and Crystal was sixteen.

In this home I learned much of the Jewish customs and life style. I learned to wash the milk dishes and meat dishes in separate washings and to put them into separate cupboards. The Sabbath began on Friday night at sundown. Mrs. Seigle and I cooked and cleaned all day on Friday. At sundown, Mrs. Seigle set two lighted candles in the west window, then took a large clean white dishtowel and covered her head and shoulders and bent over to pray. After the prayer was over she told me to sit down and be the first one to eat. She dished up beef borscht, gefilte fish, roast chicken, boiled potatoes, and Jewish Sabbath bread. She waited on me while I ate and kept insisting I eat more. I thought she had to be the world's best Jewish cook.

Segals had company from Chicago that summer. Rosie, a boarder in the home and myself were asked to give up our rooms to the guests. The boys, Leonard and Oscar, laid our their bed rolls on the sleeping porch. Rosie and I were assigned to the boys room.

On the first night of the new arrangement I went to bed early. Relaxing in the boys big double bed I fell into a sound sleep. Several hours later I was awakened by someone getting into bed with me. My first thought was, "the boys have forgotten where they are supposed to sleep." I began to kick and push. I heard a girl giggling. Rosie was hanging on to the edge of the bed about to fall out. "Is that you, Rosie?" I asked. "I thought it was one of the boys." I helped her into bed. Rosie was weak from laughing. I could not share her mirthful moments. I looked upon it as a serious encounter. The next morning Rosie got up early and went down to breakfast. I came into the kitchen a few minutes later. Rosie was eagerly telling of last nights episode — everyone was laughing. Mr. Segal looked at me with a merry grin. "Well, Gracie," he said. "I know now that my boys are safe with you." I was totally embarrassed.

Mrs. Segal was not well that summer. She had a continual backache. She and Mr. Segal were not getting along well. She seemed to be always angry with him. One night when he came home late from his work as a salesman in a men's clothing store, Mrs. Segal heard him coming and slipped out the back door. She told me she was going next door to the Goldstines. She told me to give Mr. Segal his dinner. While I was setting his food on the table, Mr. Segal said to me, "Gracie, can you tell me what is wrong with Mrs. Segal?" "Mrs. Segal isn't well," I answered. "She has a constant backache. Mr. Segal jumped up from the table and bolted out the back door. Sitting in Mrs. Goldstines kitchen he found Mrs. Segal pouring out her troubles. He took her by the hand and led her gently home. They walked through the kitchen and into the living room. There they sat down on the davenport and talked out their misunderstandings.

I thought it was time to retire to my room. I picked up my Bible and opened to Ephesians. I came upon these words in Chapter Five and Verse Thirty-one. "For this cause a man shall leave his father and mother and shall cleave to his wife and the two shall become as one flesh."

GRANDMOTHER'S STORIES

A NEW PRESIDENT

Franklin Roosevelt was elected president in 1932. His inauguration took place on March 4. I remember so well hearing him on the radio and being impressed with his charismatic personality. He was the man for the hour. Our country was writhing in the pathos of the Great Depression. This was the man with The New Deal.

First on the agenda was the Bank Holiday. All banks were closed for reorganization. Roosevelt then authorized the Civil Conservation Corps. The CCC recruited young men from the city streets to work at building parks and roads and planting trees. Boys from the sidewalks of Chicago, New York, and Minneapolis were bussed in and dumped into the Minnesota wilderness. Boys from our own small towns were there, too, living in tents while they built their barracks. Their pay checks were sent home to their families.

Works Progress Administration was organized for fathers at home. They worked on roads, built large dams and bridges. Surplus commodities were issued. Powdered milk and eggs, rice, flour, corn meal and dried fruit were welcomed at the tables of many homes. Roosevelt reached out to the very bottom of the pile. The disheartened, discouraged, the crippled, the sick, the depressed — none were left out. On March 23, 1933, President Roosevelt began his fireside chats. He outlined to the people his plans for his country. Everyone listened and knew at last that someone was taking an active interest in them. The Great Depression was now in its fourth year, and up to this time nothing had been done to relieve the suffering. Roosevelt served sixteen years in the oval office. We went with him through the Great Depression and World War II. I was shocked and disappointed when I heard of the beer party on the White House lawn. "It was only three percent beer," they said, "and beer was going to be legalized now." No longer would it hide in the mountain stills and home cellars. It was brought out in the open and served on the White House lawn. The lowly hamburger showed up at the party, too. Today the hamburger is king

GRACE CLEMENSON

Children of Jim and Gurine Clemenson; Jim, Ellen, Gerhart, Grace and Gustav.

The Clemensons; James, Dora, Ellen, Gustav, James Sr., Gurine, Gerhart and Grace. Seated: Lois, Phyllis and Leroy, 1939.

GRANDMOTHER'S STORIES

HITCHHIKING HOME

Toward the end of the summer of 1934 mother wrote that she wanted to see us before school started. She said that daddy was operating a sawmill and she was there cooking for the hired hands. She said that Elsie and Vern were with them. She wanted us to take the bus to Glenwood and Guy, our cousin, would meet us there in his old Model T. He would take us on to Gonvick. This sounded like a lark, and we were all for it. The date was set to leave. We were packed and ready with the help and blessing of our Jewish friends.

The day before we were to leave another letter came from mother saying, "Don't come." Something had happened. Daddy had left again. Mother was pregnant. They had no place to go. We were crushed.

When school started that fall I registered at South High in Minneapolis. I found a home with the Luger family who were owners and operators of the Luger Furniture Factory. They were a friendly family and paid me a dollar a week, for which I was very grateful. There were three children in this family, and we all got along well together. Mrs. Luger, too, allowed me to give little parties for my girl friends. She talked with me and helped me to feel at home. I appreciate that now.

Mother wanted Crystal and me home for Christmas that year. She and Vern had rented a little house on an acreage near Gonvick. Vern had quit school and was working to support mother and Elsie. George was born on January twenty-seventh of that winter.

Mother wrote to Crystal and me and said that she had arranged a ride for us to Gonvick with friends who were driving from Minneapolis to Gonvick for Christmas. I talked to Lugers and they agreed to let me go. The day before we were to leave another letter came from mother saying that the plans had fallen through and we would not get home for Christmas. By this time Crystal and I were becoming discouraged and depressed with the ever-failing plans to see our family. We were always a little lonely. The hope and courage for our week came from mother's regular letters. The little tunnel of light in our life always led to seeing our mother again.

One day after Christmas I said to Crystal, we are going to spend the summer with mother this summer and no one is going to say, "Don't come." We will pack up our belongings and hitchhike home. We will take them by surprise. So we began our secret plans for our two hundred and fifty mile journey. No one must know what we planned to do, for if anyone found out, our trip would end there.

Hitchhiking was severly frowned upon in those days, and considered a dangerous mode of travel.

It is now the spring of 1935. Crystal graduated from Central High. School was out for the summer. We quickly packed our belongings and set out on our trip. On our way out of town, we stopped to say goodbye to Ruth. If she was shocked at our announcement, she did not show it. She gave us her blessing and made up a package of sandwiches for our lunch. We left her with the promise that we would send her a card when we reached home to let her know of our safe arrival.

We took the bus to Columbia Heights, the end of the line. After paying our bus fare we had twenty-six cents left for the trip. This did not worry us. It is surprising how little money meant to us in those depression days. Food was our main concern and didn't we have some donuts, sweet rolls, and Ruth's sandwiches. And didn't we expect to be home that night?

When we reached the end of the bus line we walked to the highway, put down our luggage, and sat down on it. We waited for what seemed a very long time. We began to wonder if our plan was going to work, as car after car went by. At about noon an old Model A Ford came to a stop in front of us. A little old driver put his head out the window and looked us over. "Girls," he said, "I don't drive very fast but if you want to go my speed you are welcome to ride." We were anxious to be moving at any speed. We put our baggage on the back seat and climbed in on top. When he said he didn't drive very fast he put it mildly. We rode all the rest of the day at the rate of twenty-five miles an hour. At six o'clock we came to the little railroad town of Pine River. The old man, who had not spoken a word all afternoon stopped the car and said, "Well, girls, this is as far as I go." He opened the door and let us out.

We sat on our luggage and looked around. Main Street was in front of us. The city park was to our right. This certainly wasn't where we expected to spend the night. Our driver had driven off. We felt utterly alone and lonely. We walked through the park and finally decided that this was where we would stay for the night. We sat down on a park bench to wait for the sun to go down. We took an inventory of our lunch box. We had only one sandwich apiece left and two cinnamon rolls. We had been dipping frequently into our goodies all afternoon. Perhaps partly to relieve the boredom of the long, slow ride and partly to relieve the growling of our stomachs. We decided to finish off the two sandwiches for our supper and save the rolls for breakfast. We ate the sandwiches and drank water from the town pump. Then we waited for the dark. We kept very quiet for we did not want to be discovered by the police or noticed by any towns people. We were quite relieved that we did not see or come in contact with any of the Pine River citizens while we were guests of their park.

While darkness was closing in around us we made up our beds. We took our winter coats and spread them on the ground. We put on all our sweaters and long underwear and woolen socks. We lay down and spread our spring coats over us. We were glad we each had a pillow to put under our head, though before morning they became covers to seal out the creeping chill. Darkness covered us like a concealing mantle. We felt safe now and nestled our faces into our feather pillows. Sleep did not come easy but we were tired and drifted off. The night turned cold. We woke up in the early morning hours, rearranged our pillows and bed and tried for more sleep. How we welcomed the warm rays of the early morning sun. We got up and sat on the park bench for a while to absorb the warmth. We ate our breakfast and drank water from the pump. We brushed our teeth, washed our faces, and combed our hair. We packed our night clothes and we were ready to go.

We walked to the highway. This time we did not have long to wait. A shiny new Plymouth, the first car of the morning, stopped in front of us. The driver was smiling and friendly and asked us if we would like a ride. Of course that is just what we were waiting for. We were soon settled and on our way again. The driver was curious about us, and asked many questions. We told him our story. He asked us if we had had our breakfast. We said, "Yes," thinking of our rolls and water. He said, "Well, I don't know how you could. There are no cafes open yet." After about an hour of driving we found a cafe open. He stopped the car and said, "Come on, girls. We are going in for breakfast." He ordered eggs, hash browns, toast, and milk. We ate like two hungry girls at a picnic.

After several more hours of driving, we came into Bemidji. We stopped at a station for gas, our driver talked with the attendant. Together he and our host arranged for a ride for us to Bagley. We had a short wait there for our car to leave, but soon we were on our way again. We arrived in Bagley some time that afternoon. We were now only thirty miles from home. We carried our luggage to the outskirts of town. Again we sat down to wait. Now we were getting anxious to get home. It had been four years since we had been with our family. We knew our dad would not be there, but we would soon see mother, Elsie, Vern, and George, the new baby. We were getting excited at the thought. Questions entered our minds: Would they be changed? Would they be shocked to see us? Would they be happy? How would they accept their two bold hitchhikers?

As we sat there on our luggage we had time to think, for car after car went by and didn't seem to see us. Finally a car came toward us and it seemed it would also pass us by. Suddenly Crystal jumped up, stepped out into the road, and put out her thumb. At that the car came to a sudden halt. An unfriendly face peered out the window. He frowned and looked uncertain. Girl hitchhikers were rare in those days, and were very much frowned upon. Finally the car door opened and we were told to get in. The stern man at the wheel lectured and scolded us all the way to Gonvick. We listened and said nothing, for after all he was taking us home. We didn't know him but my mother did. He was her neighbor. He dropped us off on her doorstep.

What excitement! They all came running. There was hugging and kissing and crying. Mother hadn't changed. She had the same golden brown hair, hazel eyes, and big smile. I still thought she had to be the most beautiful woman in the world. Elsie was a beautiful child of eight with natural curly platinum blond hair. Vern had grown into a rugged responsible young man of sixteen. We were delighted with the baby who was five months old. We all tried to talk at once. They had many questions to ask, and we had a lot to tell. After a satisfying meal of mother's home-made bread, garden vegetables and rhubarb sauce we were put to bed for a good night's rest.

We were all happy to be together, but the next morning mother told us that Vern was supporting the family, and Crystal and I would have to go out and find work as soon as possible. We understood this. Crystal went to town the next day and got a job at Martin Martin's Cafe. She worked days and could be at home every night. I went to Bagley to work in a motherless home, caring for two boys. I had weekends off, and made a beeline home every Friday night. On Sunday night I would be in town on time to catch the CCC truck back to Bagley.

The summer passed in work and play. Crystal and I would sometimes date for Saturday night dances. These were all night affairs. We had no thought of going home before sunrise. When the dances were over at one o'clock, we climbed into cars and went to our favorite cafe for lunch. There we found nickelodeons to play, coffee and pop to drink, and friends to greet. The cafes were popular meeting places after dances, and we usually made the rounds of two or three before taking the homeward trail. At home we found mother getting breakfast. We sat down to the table and ate again. The morning was spent visiting with mother and filling her in on the evening's activities.

In September Crystal went to North Dakota to visit relatives. Vern went to the CCC camp and I was elected to stay home with mother, Elsie and George. I was delighted with this arrangement. I was a senior in high school and got a job in the school library. I worked one hour after school each night, and so was able to help at home and pay my own expenses.

We lived out of town, and Elsie and I had a mile to walk to school. These were happy times for us as we walked together in all kinds of weather, swinging our lunch pails. We were given an hour lunch break, and many times in nice weather we would run home and have lunch with mother. We could run a mile in ten minutes. Mother would have our lunch ready, and we had a half hour of companionship before running back to school. This was the highlight of my day. I wasn't enjoying school that year. I knew I had to stay with it and graduate if I wanted to go to college. College had been my goal since my freshman year.

At the Gonvick High School we had no choice of subjects. I had to take a language; French was the only one offered. I was hard-of-hearing, and it seemed that I just couldn't understand the teacher. I never did learn to speak French but my understanding of the reading and written work was good, so I got by.

Chemistry was another bug-a-boo for me. I learned it, but didn't like it. I somehow made a C. My other subjects were language, reading, and math. These came easy. My work after school in the library was a joy. I worked with one of the teachers, and we sorted, catalogued, and mended books. I always loved books and it was like working with friends.

Once each month our class was excused from study hall to have a class meeting. The business of the first meeting was to elect class officers. For some reason they had their eyes on me for president. I stood up to explain that the president should be someone who grew up with the class. The more I talked the more votes I gained and to my amazement I became class president. I found myself calling meetings to order and struggling to keep the discipline. I was amazed at how many spit balls could be exchanged by seniors. The process of conducting business was very slow. We chose our class colors, blue and yellow. We chose our motto. We poured over catalogues and picked out class rings. We planned class parties and our spring banquet. I prepared the president's speech to be given at the banquet. All in all it was a learning experience for me.

I continued to get dates for Saturday night dances. A handsome red-headed Norwegian began focusing attentions on me. He wasn't a stranger, for he was a cousin of my cousins and I had known him or of him for many years. Now I saw him with new eyes. He was two years older than I. He was six feet tall and good looking with his sharp blue eyes and dark red hair. He worked with his dad in law enforcement work as a deputy sheriff. Gerhart Cornelius Clemenson later became my husband and he stayed with law enforcement all of his life.

Gerhart and his dad had a good relationship and worked well together. The significance of this relationship was that dad owned a Model A Ford coupe. Gerhart was always able to borrow the car for our weekend projects. Skunk hunting was a favorite Sunday night activity in the fall of the year. Gerhart would borrow the car, drive out and pick me up and away we would go on a skunk hunting trip.

To hunt skunks we each had to have a good stout club. As we drove slowly along a country road, we kept a sharp eye out for skunks. They were out prowling around this time of the year in search of a winter den. When we spied a skunk, Gerhart stopped the car and we jumped out carrying our clubs. The trick of the game was to keep in front of the skunk. He, on the other hand, would keep turning around trying to focus his tail on us. If he succeeded in this, he would spray us with his stinking, choking scent. Then the game was over and he would be the winner. So, we kept dancing around and around, hitting him on the head and trying to kill him as quickly as we could. There was a bounty on skunks, and Gerhart would skin them out the next day and collect the money.

Though jobs were scarce and money hard to come by, Gerhart was always busy working at full time and part time jobs. He was never idle. He liked to come to our house on Saturday mornings for breakfast, always with a box of candy under his arm. He hauled and chopped wood for our stoves and shoveled snow. In the evening we took Mother, Elsie, and George with us and went visiting relatives. My Mother's sister lived near us and we had many fun times with their large family. Uncle John liked to call for square dances. It was a favortie past-time on a Saturday night, to push back the table and chairs and clear the kitchen for square dancing. We wound up the phonograph and put on our square dance record. Then choose your partner and do-si-do. The dance was on.

Uncle John had a sleigh and a fast team, and that meant Saturday night sleigh ride parties. Mothers and fathers, sisters and brothers, aunts, uncles and cousins were all included. We sailed across the snow on bright moon-lit nights, singing, laughing, and snuggling in the hay. School Christmas programs were popular events. These we attended, traveling by horse and sled. Christmas fooling was an old country custom during the Christmas season. The trick was to disguise ourselves in masks and costumes so we could not be recognized. We would drive quietly up to a neighbor's house and tie up the team. Then we walked up to the door and without knocking, we pushed open the door and walked in. We looked very weird in our costumes and our hosts pretended to be very frightened. They spent the next half hour trying to guess who we were, while we sat around the room daring not to say a word and give ourselves away. They were not allowed to touch us or look under our masks. After a time we were all identified and we took off our masks and lunch was served. Christmas season continued on until New Years. On New Year's Eve we celebrated again with a neighborhood dance at the town hall. Gerhart's mother cooked New Year's Day dinner. The holidays were over.

Winter passed swiftly. After New Year's, we settled down to cold, ice, and snow. Social activities reached a low ebb. Elsie and I walked our mile to school morning and night with boots, mittens, caps, jackets, and snow pants. Mother tied scarves tightly over our faces with only peep holes for our eyes. We stumbled along, carrying our books and lunch pails.

In the spring, Gerhart began to talk of marriage. He gave me an engagement ring. I kept it two weeks and gave it back. I wasn't ready for marriage. Gerhart left then and went west to find work. After graduation, I took the train to Minneapolis. Gerhart and I continued to write, and twice he came to Minneapolis to see me. Crystal was in Minneapolis again and had a job waiting for me. She was working in a Jewish orphanage. There was an opening there for me. I began working with the child psysiologist in the recreation department. There were about thirty children in the home with ages from four years old to fourteen. They were orphans and children from divided homes. There were many problems. We stayed there for the summer. In September we registered and were accepted at the University of Minnesota. We had saved money for books and tuition, and found homes near the campus where we worked for our room and board. I went to college for two quarters and had no more money for tuition. I found a full-time job in a cafe.

Grace Johnston and Ellen Clemenson, 1935.

Gustav Clemenson on the Munsrud Farm, Gonvick, Minnesota.

GRACE CLEMENSON

Gerhart and Grace Clemenson, wedding picture, August, 1938.

Grace and Gerhart Clemenson and their wedding cake made by Gerhart's mother.

GRANDMOTHER'S STORIES

"OUR WEDDING"

I began answering ads for waitress work. After going from one job to another, I finally found a nice opening in a tea room. The clientele was made up of business girls in uptown offices. I waited on tables and did cashiering. During this time Gerhart and I were writing long, serious and loving letters. We knew marriage was not far off. One day he came into the tea room where I was working. I dropped my tray and flew into his arms. The girls all watched and giggled. "Girls," I said, "This is the boy I am going to marry." Their response was, "Oh, goodie, we're going to give you a shower."

So an August date was set. Gerhart was twenty-four and I was twenty-two. We continued to work and plan for our wedding. Ruth was not about to be left out. She arranged for an August vacation. On August fifteenth, Ruth, Pearl, Oscar Jr., Crystal and I set out for Gonvick. Gerhart met us as we drove into town. We all went out to Mother's. There was much talk and plans to be made for the wedding.

Gerhart had the license and the rings. We made a shopping trip to Bemidji. Aunt Laura had a neighborhood quilting bee and presented us with a beautiful blue and white quilt. Another bridal shower was given by my girl friends in Gonvick. There was a community wedding shower for both of us at the Legion Hall. On August thirty first, 1938 we were married in the Lutheran parsonage. Crystal was my bridesmaid and Jim, Gerhart's brother, was best man. My brother, Vern was our attendant. After the knot was tied and the rice was thrown Gerhart and I escaped on a three-day honeymoon to the Lake Superior wilderness.

The celebrating was not over. When we returned home, mother and Ruth gave us a wedding reception in the Legion Hall. Gerhart's mother baked the wedding cake, a beautiful three-tier pink and white delight. Friends brought wedding gifts and lunch was served. Someone came with a violin and an accordian and with Gerhart's sister at the piano, the music began. I don't know how long the party lasted. Gerhart and I left early. In September Gerhart gave the customary expected wedding dance in the town hall. He hired a band out of Thief River to play. A collection was taken up for us, and after all expenses were paid, we had a nice little sum for our own use.

Daddy, who did not wish to be outdone, gave us an oil painting for a wedding gift. He and an Indian friend at Red Lake were making the pictures to sell. Daddy made the frame, which consisted of a slab cut cross-wise from an oak log. The bark was left on for decoration. The Indian painted a picture of a river scene with a boat and fisherman. Daddy then took the pictures and left them at a drug store in Bemidji to be sold. We were delighted to have one.

Dora Clemenson, Elsie Johnston and Phyllis Clemenson, 1934.

Gerhart's owls at the C.C.C. Camp, 1932.

One of the first C.C.C. Camps when the boys lived in tents about 1932.

GRANDMOTHER'S STORIES

LIFE AT CLEARWATER LAKE

We have now reached the fall of 1938. The economic depression had reached its lowest ebb. Jobs were scarce and Gerhart was searching for any kind of work.

Uncle Carl knew Mr. McCrady, a man from Plummer, who owned several acres of timber land in the Clearwater Lake area. He was looking for a man to do some cutting. He couldn't pay wages, he said, but he would open a charge account at the local grocery store for anyone who would take the job. There was a house on the place and Gerhart accepted the job. We moved in.

We had no furniture and no curtains. But this was not a serious handicap. I made the curtains and Gerhart bought lumber and nails and built and painted our furniture. He measured sawed and hammered. Soon we had a cupboard, table and benches. He built a wash stand with a towel rack and medicine cabinet. I was busy with a paint brush painting everything white. Last of all, Gerhart cut and put together a pretty little octagon bedside table which I painted green. I dyed the curtains green and we had Aunt Laura's pretty blue and white quilt for our bed, and braided rugs for our floor. Our first home was established. We were happy, cozy and comfortable.

One evening when Gerhart came in from his work in the woods, hungry as usual, he found no supper ready. The fires were out and I was in bed. I had been sick to my stomach all day. On the second day I was no better. Gerhart stayed in the house with me all day. He said he knew exactly what was wrong. When a married woman is sick like this, it is a sure sign she is going to have a baby. He made me stay in bed, fed me crackers and tea and kept a close eye on me. He was visibly disappointed when, in a few days, I was well and insisted on getting out of bed.

November was hunting season for deer. We spent many days tramping through the woods with our guns. We were never able to catch up with a deer or to even see one. On the last day of hunting season, we were up early, determined to get a deer. At noon we went to the house for lunch. After our lunch, we laid down for an hour's rest. After naps we dressed and went outdoors. There, under our bedroom window, were the tracks of two deer that had walked past our window while we were sleeping. I am sure they had been watching us and were checking to see why we weren't out looking for them.

One cold winter night at about midnight, Gerhart and I were awakened out of a good sound sleep by noisy shouting and banging on our door. Gerhart opened the door and there was his brother Gus. Dad Clemenson had sent him in the Model A

Ford to bring us home for Christmas. We built up the fire and while Gus warmed up with a cup of hot coffee, we dressed in our warmest clothes. Soon we were on our way. We had a wonderful visit, dividing our time with our two families. Christmas Eve we all got together with Gerhart's family. On Christmas Day we were with mother and Vern, Elsie and George.

On January third, Dad Clemenson loaned us his Model A to drive back to Clearwater Lake. Gerhart's brother Jim went with us and stayed until Spring. He went to the woods with Gerhart every day to help with the cutting. We rearranged our house when Jim moved in. Gerhart and I took the upstairs bedroom. This room was cold and drafty. Through the cracks in the wall we could look out and watch the stars. On stormy nights the snow blew in making drifts on the window sill.

The winter was spent quietly. On Monday I melted snow in our copper boiler and did the washing on the washboard. I hung clothes in the woodshed to dry. On Tuesday I ironed with a sad iron heated on top of the stove. I baked bread on Wednesday. On Friday I cleaned the house and on Saturday I baked Boston brown bread and baked beans for our Saturday night supper. I learned to bake good chocolate cakes in my wood stove oven. There is a trick in knowing how many sticks of wood to burn to get the right temperature for pies, cakes and bread.

On Saturday nights we took our baths and dressed up. On this night we had a standing invitation to spend the evening with our neighbors, the Genzels. We played cards and listened to barn dance music on their radio. Mrs. Genzel always had a delicious lunch of sandwiches, wild raspberry sauce, freshly baked cinnamon rolls and coffee. At midnight we walked the mile-and-a-half home in the moonlight with the crunch, crunch, crunch of the snow under our feet. On Sunday night we were often invited back for supper and to enjoy Amos and Andy and Fibber McGee and Mollie on the radio.

The winter was cold and rugged that year. We had two heavy snow storms that kept us snow bound for several weeks. At times like these we all ran out of groceries and began our neighborhood bartering. Old George had a good supply of potatoes in his root cellar. We had a supply of red beans. Neighbor John had milk and eggs. The Genzels usually had everything. Everyone kept in touch with everyone. No one went hungry. Gerhart had a quarter in money, the only money we saw all winter. We kept it in a sugar bowl in the cupboard. It was handy to have in case of an emergency. One day I took the quarter and walked to Genzel's to buy a bag of tea. They did not want my money. I came home with the tea and put the quarter back in the sugar bowl. One night I made pancakes for supper. We had butter to put on them, but no syrup. Jim took the quarter and ran to Neighbor John's to buy a cup of sugar. He came running back, put the quarter back in ths sugar bowl and made some sugar syrup. We all sat down to eat. Jim reached for the syrup and accidentally knocked the pitcher over. The syrup ran all over the table and down on the floor. I remember how heart sick we felt as we watched the syrup drip off the edge of the table. Poor Jim thought he just couldn't eat pancakes without syrup. He did that day. Hunger does strange things to our taste buds. As for the quarter, no one wanted it. It stayed in the sugar bowl all winter.

The snow was deep that winter. We had no well on our place. Our drinking water had to be carried from the well of our nearest neighbor, John, who lived a half mile from our house. Gerhart carried two pails and had to hold them up at chest level to keep them from dragging in the snow. I carried one pail, holding it up as high as I could as I waded through the fluff. On one occasion when I came up to our porch, I slipped on the ice and fell, spilling all of my water on the porch. We had a good laugh over this.

When Gerhart was a boy growing up he often helped his mother with the Christmas baking. Lefsa was a special kind of flowery flat bread made with mashed potatoes and flour. It was baked especially for Christmas Eve to be eaten with lutifisk. Gerhart wanted to perfect the art of lefsa making and carry the ritual of holiday baking into his own home. One day he boiled a kettle of potatoes. He mashed them and added some salt and butter and flour. He rolled out the dough into little balls the size of a walnut. Then with the rolling pin he rolled each one flat like a pie crust. Then he put them on a hot griddle and browned them on both sides. We all three enjoyed fresh lefsa hot off the griddle. I ate mine. It was good and flavorful, but a bit chewy. Jim took a bite of his and chewed and chewed. Gerhart got a bit huffy when Jim told him he should try selling it for shoe leather. In later years we perfected the recipe and mastered the art of lefsa making. It became a family project. As the children were growing up we set aside one day before Christmas for lefsa making. It became a part of our holiday ritual that remains to this day.

The winter was not without its excitement, however. Jim happened to be in the right place at the right time to see the burying of a body in the Clearwater River. One clear, sunny morning Jim walked two miles to Genzel's on an errand. The main road and Clearwater River ran parallel to each other through the woods. On his return home Jim took a short cut through the woods. This brought him up onto a high elevation overlooking the road and the river. He saw a car drive down the road and stop near the river. Two men got out and set a long sled on the ground. Then they opened the trunk of the car and took out what appeared to be a human body. It was long and slim and wrapped in a blanket. They laid it on the sled and both men took hold of the rope and started pulling. the sled runners cut into the snow and the body drug over the end, making a deep track as they pulled it along. The two men pulled their load off the road and out across the field to the river. There they took out an ice saw and cut and removed a round chunk of ice. Then they took the body off the sled and slid it into the hole. They replaced the cut chunk of ice in the hole and returned to their car and drove away.

Jim was standing in a position to get a good view of the whole procedure without being seen. He came home breathless and told us his story. Gerhart, Jim and I took a flashlight and a blanket and went to the river. We found the hole and took out the chunk of ice. We put the blanket over our heads and looked into the hole. All we could see was rushing water. We replaced the chunk of ice and walked over to talk to our neighbor, John. We told him our story. He advised us to keep this adventure strictly quiet. He said it was for our own safety. In those days there was bootlegging and gang wars in the big cities of Chicago and Minneapolis. Much of this crime was carried over into the small towns. None of us believed that this was a local incident. As we watched the papers we found no reports of missing local persons. Could it be that some gang-lord had ordered the death sentence of some little member who knew too much? We did not want to be among those who knew too much. We told our story to no one.

Street Scene, Gonvick, Minnesota

GRANDMOTHER'S STORIES

THE FAIRBANKS PLACE

In the spring of nineteen thirty nine we left our wilderness home at Clearwater Lake and moved to Gonvick. Gerhart got a job as a mechanic at Chet Berg's garage, and was earning twenty dollars a week. We decided we could rent a house. We found one two miles out of town which we could rent for fifteen dollars a month. Gerhart's mother told us that this house belonged to a friend of hers, Mary Fairbanks, and the farm was known as the Old Fairbank's Place.

We went to look at it and found it to be a big, old-fashioned country farm house. The big farm kitchen was at the back of the house facing the back yard. The large living room had a big picture window looking out on the apple orchard. There was one bedroom downstairs and two bedrooms upstairs. We liked the house and decided to rent it. We planned to use the living room as our kitchen, dining. and living rooms, and to set up our bed in the downstairs bedroom.

Gerhart bought a new, bright, colorful linoleum for our main room and we had braided rugs for our bedroom. We had our kitchen wood-burning stove which we brought from Clearwater Lake and which served for both cooking and heating. We found a second-hand dining room table and chairs for our dining area. We had a small table and chair and a rocking chair for our living room. Gerhart came home one night with a radio and a new Aladdin lamp to light up our hearts and home. We moved in with happy anticipations.

I cooked our first evening meal and we sat down to eat. We looked hungrily at the baked potatoes, baked beans, and home-made bread. We had just filled our plates when we heard a knock, knock, knock at the door. I opened the door, but there was no one there. I sat down and we began to eat. Again we heard three knocks on the door. Again I went to the door. Again there was no one there. We began to feel uneasy and uncomfortable. We went on with our meal. Again we heard the knock, knock, knock. This time we both got up, and Gerhart opened the door. There was no one there. We decided someone was playing a prank on us. We began to search the yard. We looked all through the orchard and around the house and in the barn. We found no one. We decided to give up and go to bed. This was only the beginning of our experiences of life in a haunted house.

Our first night was spent fighting bedbugs. We slid into our new wedding sheets and turned out our new Aladdin lamp and closed our eyes. The bedbugs had other plans for us that night. They marched out of their fort in the walls and, like a mighty army, they made war on us. A bedbug is a blood-sucking, wingless bug of reddish-brown color and vile odor. It is a carrier of dangerous diseases. They live on the blood of humans.

The next morning we were exhausted from the night-long battle. We sat down to plan our strategy. We had heard of burning sulphur for various maladies and decided to try it for bedbugs. Crystal was home from Minneapolis visiting mother. She came over for the day to help me. We went to the drug store to purchase some sulphur. We found a small cast-iron barrel and set it in the center of the room on our new linoleum. We then took some hot coals from the stove and put them in the bottom of the barrel. Crystal took the package of sulphur and opened it up. She began to sprinkle the sulphur over the coals. When the first bits of powder hit the coals they burst into flame. The paper bag caught on fire and Crystal quickly threw it aside. Burning sulphur was scattered over the linoleum. Sparks and flames were burning all around us. We quickly grabbed towels and wet them in the water pail. We hit the flames and soon the fire was out. We found a scorched spot on our new linoleum and a burned place under the barrel. That night we again shared our bed with an army of hungry bedbugs.

The next morning Gerhart went into town and talked to the druggist about our problem. Mr. Sloggerman suggested fumigation, and offered to come out the next day and do it for us. We had to vacate the house for twenty-four hours. This treatment was guaranteed to kill all bedbugs, rats, mice, flies, and mosquitoes. No mention was made of ghosts.

We soon discovered that we had a ghost who was fully determined to share our home. Or perhaps it is more accurate to say we were invading his home. I was never a believer in ghosts, but after living here a few weeks I knew that some kind of a supernatural spirit did exist. When we moved in a neighbor asked my mother how I liked living in a haunted house. My mother answered, "Whatever you do, don't tell her that house is haunted."

My little dog Chipso and I were alone together all day. Chipso was alert and sharp. She appointed herself my bodyguard and protector. Many times we heard the back door open and close and believed someone had come in. Chipso would bark and go with me to the door. Never did we find anyone there. We finally gave up the attempted greeting. We paid no attention as the door would open and close and our friend would come and go.

One night Gerhart and I were awakened from a deep sleep by the sound of clawing and scratching on the inside wall by our bed. We got up and lit the lamp. We pulled the bed out and tapped and examined both sides of the wall. There were no scratches on the wall or any sign of any little animal. We found nothing. All activity stopped while we were searching. But as soon as we got back into bed the scrathing began again and continued on into the night.

I was now about five months pregnant with our first baby. I was particular about my exercise and rest. I liked to rest in the afternoons, lying on the bed reading and sleeping. Chipso had her bed on the floor beside me. She liked to lie and doze in the quiet of the afternoon. It was not always quiet, however. We were often disturbed by the sound of footsteps going up and down the stairs. There were twelve steps in the stairway and I could count them as our friend would go up and down, and he went up and down all afternoon. Chipso would bark and run to the stairway. Together we would go upstairs to search things out. I looked in the bedrooms and in the attic. We found no clues. All activity ceased while we were making our search, but as soon as we lay down to rest the stepping began again. We were forced to give up on our rest for that afternoon.

Our ghost liked to putter around in the kitchen when we were away from home. When we arrived back we could feel his supernatural presence as we walked into the room. It was like a faint rustle or a whisper as if someone were taking a hasty leave as we came in.

One night I came into the house alone after dark. I saw a light in a crack underneath the stairwell. I watched it and wondered what it could be. I took a table knife and slid it into the crack trying to touch it. The light slid along ahead of the knife and I was never able to reach it. I thought this to be very strange and I gave up the search. I lit up our own Aladdin lamp and sat down to wait for Gerhart to come home for supper. When he looked for the light under the stairwell, it was gone. I was not especially frightened, and I learned to live with these mysterious activities. I was beginning to believe in haunted houses.

My mother and brother drove by the house one night after we had moved out. The house was all lit up. Mother asked a neighbor if someone had moved in. The neighbor answered, "No. No one lives there. We often see a light in the house at night."

During this stay in the haunted house I was happily and comfortably pregnant. Gerhart was working steadily as a mechanic at Chet Berg's garage. At the end of each month he was given the job of collecting outstanding bills and repossessing cars.

Much of his work was with the Chippewa Indians at the Indian Reservation. This job was given to Gerhart because no one else wanted it. It was challenging and dangerous. Angry Indians are dangerous enemies.

The Indians who came to town to buy cars from Chet were not mechanics. They drove their cars like they drove their horses, hard and fast. When the car broke down they did not know what to do. They left it wrecked and junked in a heap by the roadside. They also could not understand why they had to make any more payments on a car that wasn't running, and they usually refused to do so. They were very angry when Gerhart came with the towing truck to tow the car back to the garage for repairs and resale.

Gerhart was friendly and sympathetic. He learned some of their language and tried very hard to talk them into a peaceable settlement. I went with him on some of these trips. On one occasion as we were out looking for a car, we came upon a very unfriendly Indian. He was driving a car on which he had made only one payment. He had no intention of making another one. Gerhart drove up beside him. The Indian glared at us. Then he jumped out of his car carrying a gun. "You no take my car," he shouted as he pointed the gun in our direction. Gerhard walked up to him and did some very fast talking. After a lengthy conversation and firm persuasion he let us take the car. We took him to his home and towed the car back to the garage.

On another occasion Chet sent Gerhart's brother Jim and a friend on a collection trip. They saw the car they were looking for in the Indian's yard. Jim went into the house and explained his mission. He said he had come to collect on the car or repossess it. The Indian grabbed a butcher knife and swung it at Jim and yelled, "You leave my house!" Jim said, "Yes, you bet I am leaving." They drove back to the garage without the car. Jim told Chet that never again would he set foot on the Indian Reservation.

These were the Chippewa Indians. They were proud and savage. They spoke little English and could not understand white man's ways. The white man, too, could not understand their ways. There were many misunderstandings between the Indians and their white neighbors. In those early days we were well-advised to keep off the reservation.

Our baby was due in February of nineteen thirty-nine. I went regularly for my monthly check-up. I was healthy and happy and all was going well. I took long walks and often went with Gerhart on his trips as collecting agent. One week before the due date the doctor said he was going to induce labor and deliver the baby early. He had a convention in Minneapolis to attend and wanted the baby to come before he left. He gave me some medication and instructed me to leave for the hospital as soon as I felt labor coming on.

Gerhart had the car ready and running for several hours as the weather was cold and he didn't want any problems with the take-off. We left our house at four-thirty in the afternoon of February nineteenth. At five o'clock I was put to bed in the hospital. Labor continued and developed quickly. At six o'clock the nurse called the doctor and told him that the baby was coming. He was having dinner and said he would come later. He did not believe that a first baby could come this fast.

GRANDMOTHER'S STORIES

Soon I was taken to the delivery room and given a medication to halt the labor. The nurse called the doctor again. He said he was reading the evening paper and he would come when he was finished. Sometime later the nurse called the doctor again and told him to come at once, for he had lost the baby and he was about to lose the mother. The doctor then arrived and delivered my baby who had drowned in the birth water and was now dead. Kathleen Rae, my sweet little bundle of joy, was gone forever. The Lord giveth and the Lord taketh away. Gerhart wrapped her in one of her little blankets and put her in the car seat beside him. He drove twenty miles from the hospital to Gonvick. Roy Slaggerman, our good friend, the undertaker, was roused from his sleep and began his work of washing and dressing her for the funeral. Gerhart chose the casket and picked out the little clothes she would wear.

The next morning Gerhart and Jim began the long, cold job of digging the grave with pick ax and shovel. The funeral was held that afternoon. Chet closed the garage for the afternoon, and Gerhart's mother served lunch at her home. I lay in my hospital bed and never saw my baby.

Mother came to the hospital and described the casket to me. Kathleen Rae, my angel baby, lay dressed in a long white dress with matching bonnet. Her beautiful long slender fingers folded across her breast. Her sweet little sad mouth turned down, and little eyes closed. I know I will see her on that great resurrection day, when all tears shall be wiped away and there will be no more sorrow. God is so good.

Mary Johnston, Grandma Clemenson, Gurine Clemenson, Dora Clemenson. Seated: Grace Johnston, Phyllis, Lois and Grace Clemenson, 1936.

Jim and Gurine Clemenson, 1939.

GRACE CLEMENSON

Jimmy Knudsen, Oscar Backlund, 1934.

Pearl Backlund, 1937.

Ruth and Oscar Backlund, 1962.

GRANDMOTHER'S STORIES

A NEW LIFE IN IOWA

Gerhart's work as mechanic at Chet's garage had been steady. He had managed to save forty dollars. With this money he bought forty acres of land near Trail. We planned to move there some day.

Our plans changed. We decided to leave northern Minnesota. Gerhart traded the land for a Model A Ford and we began to pack. We had sixteen dollars and fifty cents to take us as far as the money would go, into an unknown journey.

Our furniture was stored in mother's big spare bedroom. Our clothes were packed in the car. Gerhart's mother made a batch of cookies and a delicious lemon pie for our lunches. Mother gave us a loaf of home-made bread and a fried chicken.

Early one morning in the first week of May, I kissed my mother good-bye, gave my mother-in-law a hug, and we left. They were not sad at our leaving, for they all said we would soon be back. It was a beautiful warm spring day and we enjoyed every mile of it. We stopped to eat our lunch underneath the shade of a big elm tree. We sat in the cool grass eating chicken with our fingers and relishing every bite. The lemon pie was oh, so good! After the pie we drank cool water from a near-by brook.

The car was running well and gave us no trouble. Gas was 30¢ a gallon and used oil was free for the asking. Water, too, was necessary and plentiful. We found it in the ditches by the side of the road. The radiator had a great thirst for water, and would steam angrily and boil in protest when dry. Gerhart carried a little can in the car, and every hour or so we stopped to fill the thirsty tank.

We were heading for Minneapolis, a distance of two hundred and fifty miles. By evening we were visiting with our friends Ruth and Oscar Backlund. Gerhart began a search for mechanic work. We stayed there several days and found no work of any kind. Gerhart's sister, Ellen, and husband Verl lived in Rochester, Minnesota. They were on vacation and had given us the keys to their apartment. We stayed several days. There was no work in Rochester. Manley, Iowa, was our next goal. Gladys and Floyd, Gerhart's cousins, lived on a farm near Grafton, Iowa. They gave us a royal welcome. Our bread and cookies, our pie and chicken, were gone, and our stomachs were empty. How we relished the steak, potatoes, and gravy they fed us. Gladys suggested that we drive on to Cedar Rapids, Iowa, and look up Uncle Clemmy and Aunt Betty.

It was a long drive to Cedar Rapids. We arrived there late one afternoon, tired, hungry, and broke. Uncle Clemmy and Aunt Betty were surprised and happy to see us. The greetings were warm and loving. Although we were perfect strangers, our name was Clemenson and that was enough for them. They took us in like the parents of long-lost children.

We arrived on Friday of Memorial Day weekend in 1940, slept, ate, and talked. Uncle Clemmy said that Laplant Choate would be hiring men the following week. This was the company where he worked and he was sure Gerhart could get work there. On Monday Gerhart put in his application. On Tuesday he joined the line-up in front of the gate. When the gate was opened he crowded in close to the door. The door opened and the boss stepped out. He announced that there would be three men hired that day. Then he pointed his finger at three men and said, "You and you and you." Gerhart was hired. He went to work the next day, joining Uncle Clemmy in the hydraulic department.

During the fall and winter of 1940 and 1941 we lived with Uncle Clemmy. In the spring of 1941 we rented a house together. Gerhart and I took the upstairs apartment. Uncle Clemmy and Aunt Betty lived downstairs. Gerhart and Uncle Clemmy worked together on the second shift. They left for work at a quarter to four and got home a little after midnight. Aunt Betty and I spent our time cooking, baking, canning, and shopping. Aunt Betty had many friends who kept dropping in. Aunt Betty had a special weakness for ice cream. Every evening we would jump in the car, take a cool ride around the countryside, and stop at Kreb's Dutch Girl for a triple dip ice cream cone.

One Saturday night Aunt Betty and I were home relaxing. It was hot and we had our fans going. There were no air conditioners in those days. I was sitting on the davenport and Aunt Betty was relaxing in her favorite chair, eating an ice cube. We had the radio on and an orchestra was playing some of our favorite barn dance tunes. Suddenly a storm hit. The wind blew a gale, lightning zig-zagged across the sky. Thunder rattled the windows. I got up and closed the door to keep out the rain. I settled back down on the davenport with a glass of ice water, relaxing and enjoying the cool temperature. Then it happened. Lightning struck a cottonwood tree outside the window behind the radio. With a crash and a flash of light the window broke and the radio exploded. I suffered a momentary blackout. When I came to I found myself sitting on the floor. Aunt Betty didn't move, but upon feeling a cold spot in her stomach, she realized she had swallowed an ice cube. We were too shaken to even look at the damage. Soon the boys came home. They patched up the window and carried the radio out to the garage. The next morning they sawed down the cottonwood tree. Cottonwood trees are known to attract electricity. It is well not to have them growing near the house.

Merle and Rose Brenniman were our very close friends. Merle was now working with Uncle Clemmy and Gerhart at Laplant Choate. Their story of the depression days still fascinates me and I must tell it here.

The Brennimans were married in 1929, the year of the stock market crash. Panic had gripped the nation. Banks closed, bankers became paupers, clients went berserk, factories laid off their workers, business went bankrupt, tramps knocked at doors asking for a handout. Men and boys rode the box cars from East to West in search of jobs. Bread lines and soup lines were familiar scenes extending for blocks in the downtown areas.

Merle and Rose continued to work. Rose was a waitress in a down-town cafe. Merle drove a cab for a taxi company. They rented a small efficiency apartment near their work. They were very frugal. Walking was their only mode of transportation. They had a dream, however, and always they could see a new car at the end of their rainbow.

Rose, one day, took a coffee can and cut a slit in the top. "From now on," she said, "our pennies and nickels will go in here and someday we will ride in our own new car."

One Saturday morning in June of 1940, Uncle Clemmy, Aunt Betty, Gerhart and I were sitting in the living room. Merle and Rose drove up in their new Buick. They had taken their cans of money to the bank that morning and had it counted out. They went to a car dealer, picked out their car, and paid eight hundred dollars in cash. This was the savings of ten years' labor. How excited we all were. The next weekend all six of us took a trip to the Wisconsin Dells in the new car. Merle was the proud and happy driver.

Betty Clemenson, Rose Brenniman, Wisconsin Dells, 1940.

GRACE CLEMENSON

Betty Clemenson, Clarence Clemenson, Wisconsin Dells, 1940.

Grace Clemenson, Gerhart Clemenson, Wisconsin Dells, 1940.

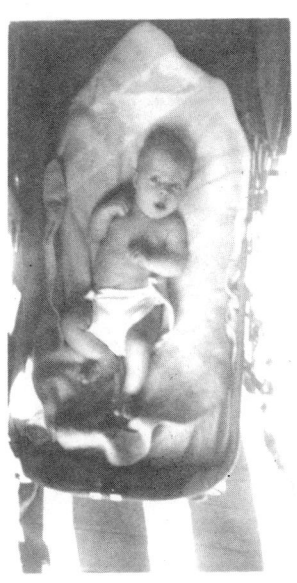

Gary Clemenson, 1942.

Vern Clemenson, 1945.

GRANDMOTHER'S STORIES

BABIES GROWING UP

In January of 1942 I was pregnant again. We were settled in an upstairs apartment in Uncle Clemmy and Aunt Betty's house. Gerhart's work was steady. The income was good. We bought our first refrigerator. We had a bed and a chest of drawers, a table and some chairs. We were comfortable. We felt quite rich. In the spring, Uncle Clemmy and Aunt Betty bought a home. We then moved to another upstairs apartment. Now we were near the city center, near the bus line and near the hospital.

On the evening of September third, Gary was born. I had been canning tomatoes all day. I had prepared our evening meal. As we began to eat, I felt my first little pain. Soon there was another and another, growing a little stronger each time. Gerhart called the doctor. We walked to the hospital as we had no car. At the hospital the elevator was full, so we walked up the stairs to the maternity ward. A nurse met me in the hall. "What are you doing here?" She asked me. "I am in labor," I answered, feeling another pain. "You don't look like it to me," she answered. "You had better go back home!" I was thankful then to see my doctor coming down the hall. He told the nurse to put me to bed. I didn't keep them waiting long. At 9:35 Gary Douglas Clemenson was born. He was a healthy eight pound five ounce boy. The striking thing about him was his beautiful red hair. He had big blue eyes that had a way of looking right at you and going straight to your heart.

Hospitalization for the birth of a baby was fourteen days. I was kept in bed and treated to bed baths, back rubs and bed pans. After a week I was allowed to sit up in a chair and walk to the bathroom. My milk was in and Gary was an eager eater. He kicked and wiggled and enjoyed every mouthful. I was given instructions on how to bathe and powder him and how to dress and feed him. I chose my pediatrician, Doctor Downing, and he came to see us. He talked to me about a date when I should bring Gary in for his first check-up.

At last one happy day Gerhart came to take us home. Gary was dressed in his new clothes and wrapped in new blankets. His daddy took him up gently and we rode home in Aunt Betty's car. I was weak and shakey. I nursed Gary and put him in his crib. Gerhart opened a jar of home-made peaches. I had peaches and bread and butter for my supper. Our first night home was a quiet one. Gary slept soundly all through the night. The one who didn't sleep was daddy. He got up every hour to peek into the crib to see if the baby was still alive. At last at six o'clock in the morning Gary began to kick and holler. He was hungry and I was glad to be relieved of some milk.

Gary grew fast and soon he was crawling on the floor. Now we began to have trouble with our neighbors - two old maid sisters who lived in the apartment below us. They began to complain to the landlady that the rocking chair made too much noise. They heard Gary when he cried. They complained when I drew water for his bath. With their broom handle they pounded on their ceiling when Gary crawled from room to room. The landlady was beside herself. She made a ruling that Gary would no longer be allowed to play in his play pen in the back yard, nor were we any longer allowed to sit on the front porch. We also began to get strange phone calls about apartments for rent. If I had said, "Yes, I am interested in looking at another apartment," she could have evicted us immediately. I knew this was a trick on her part and I would not talk to anyone on the phone about another apartment.

During the war the government set up Government Housing agencies to aid young families on the move. There were a lot of problems with landlords taking unfair advantage of the influx of young couples coming into the city.

One day I took Gary and went to the office of Government Housing. I told them my problem. They told me to try to find another place to live. They warned me not to let the landlady know we were looking or planning to move. They told me to call them as soon as we got moved. Then they said this to me, "When the landlady and those two old maids get their peace and quiet, I hope they enjoy it."

We found a house to rent and soon moved out. I called the Housing Agency and they took swift action. The two old maids were evicted. They closed up the apartment house and the land-lady was left to live there alone. It was some time before she was allowed to rent the apartment out again. Soon we moved into a rented house with a kitchen, dining room, living room and three bedrooms all furnished. We had plenty of room and my mother was able to pay us an extended visit. We enjoyed a quiet winter.

In the spring of 1943 we moved again. The house across the street from us came up for sale. The young man who owned it was drafted into the Army and, as was the usual case, given three weeks in which to settle up his business and leave. He had to sell at once, and he offered us the home and all the furniture for four thousand dollars. This was a buy, but the catch was we did not have any money. We needed several hundred dollars for a down payment, and we had no way to get it. We needed the money immediately. Gerhart talked it over with Max, the head foreman at the plant. Max said, "You want that house awfully bad, don't you?" Gerhart said, "Yes, you bet I do!" Max said, "Come to my house tomorrow morning at nine o'clock and I will have the money for you. We were there on time.

GRANDMOTHER'S STORIES

On entering the front door we saw a huge safe sitting in the living room. Max worked the combination and the door flew open. To our amazement we saw hundreds of bills all stacked neatly in little compartments. Max counted out the amount we needed for the down payment and handed it to us. He told us to pay it back however and whenever we could. There would be no interest charge.

Gerhart and I hurried to the bank as this was the final day for closing the deal. We signed all the papers and the house was ours. Nothing left to do now but to get moved in and keep up the payments. For a long time we skimped and saved. We paid our friend Max a payment each month and the bank got a payment. On arriving home after our day at the bank, we began to plan our move into our first home. We did not have much to move, and we did not have to move far. The next morning we began carrying our belongings across the street. We spent all day running back and forth. Last of all we picked up Gary, his blanket and teddy bear, carried him across the street and set him down in his own home. We were settled, for everything we needed was there. The refrigerator and stove were in place with kitchen bar and stools. In the living room we had two davenports and a drop-leaf table and chairs. To add to this was a brick fireplace at one end of the long, spacious living room. Although this was a small, one bedroom cottage, to us it was a castle. We had a lot-and-a-half of spacious yard. A tool shed stood at the end of the yard and Gerhart soon had a sandbox in place and a swing up. He built a picnic table and benches and we planted a garden. There were several big elm trees in the yard and an apple tree. I planted flowers in the front window flower boxes. It was all very pretty and lovely. Far beyond our wildest dreams.

Gary was two years old when we took him to the hospital for a lengthy operation. He was an active baby. At a year-and-a-half he was climbing on everything. The higher he could get, the better he liked it. I even found him sitting on top the piano one time. One day he pushed a chair over to the sink where I was washing dishes. He splashed in the water awhile, then picked up a glass. He turned around and stepped off the chair. He fell on the floor with his hand and the glass under him. The glass broke and cut his right hand at the base of his little finger. I had just taken a course in Red Cross first aid and home-nursing. I had learned about bandaging cuts and bruises. I washed off the blood and stopped the bleeding. I put a wad of gauze over the cut and doubled up his hand and put a bandage on it. In a few days I changed the bandage. In another week it was healed . The little finger did not look right. I saw that he had no control over it. He could not open it. When I pulled it open he could not shut it. I took him to the doctor and found that Gary had cut the cord in his little finger. An operation would be necessary to tie it up. Gary was on the operating table for two-and-a-half hours. The doctor had just given up on finding the little white cord, no bigger than a hair, and was planning to amputate the finger, when he found the cord lodged in the wrist.

This was war time. There was a shortage of nurses in our hospitals. I was asked to stay with him, and was given a cot to sleep on. I performed small nursing chores and helped him with his meals and toilet. I washed his hands and face and changed his gown. Gary had a brown corduroy hat which he insisted on wearing all day. A little shock of red hair kept peeping out. His big blue eyes sparkled. In his long white hospital gown he looked like a litte red-headed angel. He was the pet of the children's ward. We stayed for two days and were discharged. We went home with splints and bandages. We were cautioned to be very careful with the damaged hand. The next day, however, Gary forgot and swung the splint around and hit a playmate on the head. Gary walked into the house looking very smug. His playmate went home crying.

On April 29, 1945, Vern Merrill was born. He weighed nine pounds and two-and-a-half ounces and was twenty one inches tall. His entrance into the world was quick and easy. He was a healthy and contented baby. I had a good supply of mother's milk, and he was an eager eater. We stayed in the hospital the appointed fourteen days. Mother came to be with me and to care for Gary while I was in the hospital.

World War II continued on. Gerhart was a night foreman at LaPlant Choat and worked twelve to fourteen hours a day. We had no car and depended on buses for transportation. We stayed close to home and planned our own recreation. Our big back yard with swings and picnic table was the center of many picnics. Clemmy and Betty came often and Merle and Rose were frequent visitors. Ruth Pritchard worked as a dispatch clerk and she and her mother lived near us. Ruth visited us often. Ruth later became my sister-in-law.

In March of 1945 Clemmy and Betty adopted a little daughter. They named her Patty Jo. We saw a lot of Patty and have many pictures of her and Vern growing up together and many good memories. On Vern's second birthday I planned a party. Vern was talking well and he also liked to sing. When we sang his birthday song he joined in with a loud and lusty voice singing, "Happy Birthday to Me." This brought a chuckle from the grown-ups. Vern grew tall and lanky. He had serious gray-green eyes and blonde hair. He was a quiet and sensitive child.

JoAnn was born on August 25, 1948. My brothers Vern and George were visiting me and extended their visit until after her birth. Gerhart was working long hours and was seldom home. We were so happy to welcome our baby girl. I had dreamed of having a little girl, but did not dare to plan on it. Now she was here. JoAnn was an angel, so smiling and so happy. She came with blonde hair, blue eyes and rosy cheeks. She weighed nine pounds and one ounce. She was active and bouncy. How we loved her! JoAnn became a healthy, active two-year old. Her sleep habits were good and she liked to go to bed early and get up early.

One morning very early before I was up, the doorbell rang. Mrs. Miller, my neighbor down the street, was my caller. "You had better come and see what JoAnn is doing," she said. I hurried to dress and walked up to Mrs. Miller's house. Out in the street I saw JoAnn. She was lying in her little wagon wrapped up in her blanket watching the cars go by. I picked her up and, pulling the wagon, we walked home. JoAnn was about three years old when she began to outgrow her nap time. One afternoon I put her to bed for her nap. Later when I checked on her, she was not in her bed. I found her six blocks away playing on the swings on the school playground. The next day I again put her down for her nap. I checked on her again and again she was gone. The window of her bedroom was open. I looked out and saw a pillow on the ground under the window. I knew how she was getting out. She opened the window, threw out a pillow, and jumped out to a soft landing. I found her again at the school playground, swinging on the swings.

One day JoAnn came into the kitchen and asked me for a pencil and paper. She sat down and scribbled and scribbled. She folded it up and asked me if she could mail her letter. I told her that she could. She left the room and I didn't see her for some time. Soon Mrs. Miller knocked on the back door. "Do you know where JoAnn is?" she asked. "Well, no, I guess I don't. She was in the kitchen awhile ago." I replied. "I just saw her at the post office. She was going in as I was going out," Mrs. Miller said. I walked to the post office to meet her, and found she really meant it when she said she was going to mail a letter. JoAnn and I liked to wear mother-daughter dresses. I made two sets of matching dresses for us when she was small.

John was born on February 14, 1951 at one o'clock in the morning. He weighed seven pounds, twelve ounces, and was twenty-one inches long. We named him John Joseph, not for any particular person, but because I liked the nickname Johnny Joe. Johnny Joe became his name until he started school and requested that we begin calling him John. "Johnny Joe is for babies," he said. Johnny Joe was the delight of our family. He was bouncy, healthy, and happy. He held the family under his spell. He was the master of his little realm. JoAnn was three-and-one-half years old when Johnny Joe was born. She liked to help with his bath. She liked to count his toes and powder his tummy. She sat in the big arm chair, propped up with pillows, feeding him his orange juice. When we got him to bed for his nap, JoAnn and I would busy ourselves preparing lunch. JoAnn liked to set the table, pretending the knives were the daddys and the forks were the mothers and the spoons were the children. There were six in our family now, four children and a mother and daddy. When Johnny

GRACE CLEMENSON

Joe began to walk, I bought him a pair of red bib trousers. I had his name printed on the bib. He liked to wear them to church. At church one morning I was asked to go up on the rostrum and give a reading. Johnny Joe, who was sitting with Gary, got away, and started down the aisle. He had his eye on me and came straight for me. He walked up two steps to the rostrum, put both arms around my knees and hung on. Nothing could distract him. Everyone laughed. He was the darling of the church from that time on.

John was four-and-a-half years old when he was hospitalized and operated on for a hernia. He had been kicked in the groin by a little playmate. Gerhart and I went to the hospital to see him the day after the operation. We carried him to the playroom and found a book to read. We left finally and were walking down the hall when we heard a little voice behind us. John had climbed out of the crib and came running after us calling, "I go wiff you, muvver, daddy. I go wiff you." We picked him up and put him back in his crib. He cried so hard I decided not to go back. Gerhart went every morning and evening. I went up to take him home. He had been hospitalized for five days. I had a special cake decorated just for him. It was a grand homecoming.

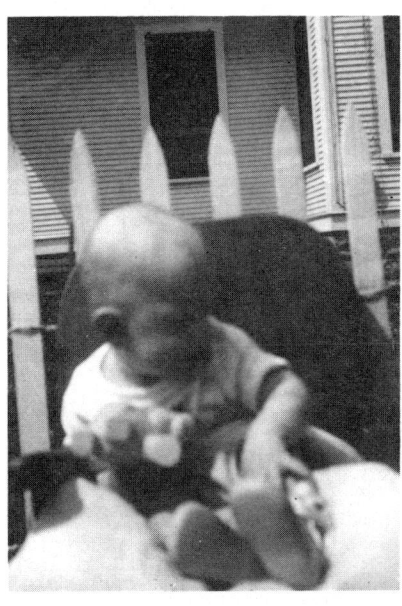

John Clemenson, 1951.

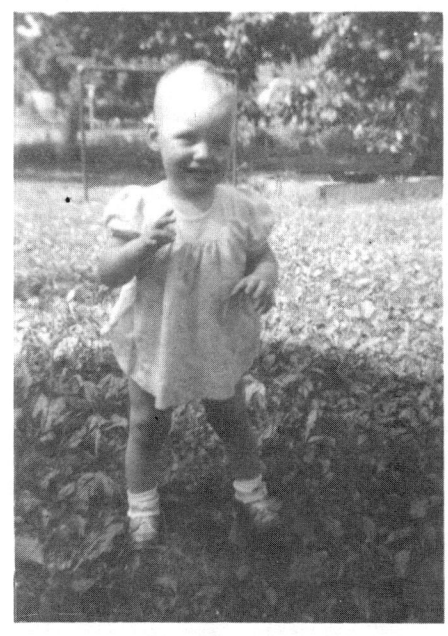

JoAnn Clemenson, 1948.

GRANDMOTHER'S STORIES

Clarence and Betty Clemenson with Patty Jo.

Betty Clemenson with Patty Jo.

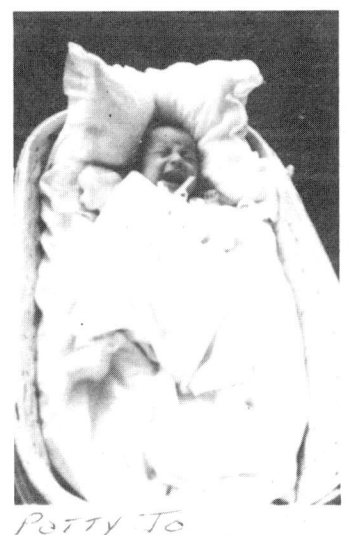

Patty Jo Clemenson, 1945.

GRACE CLEMENSON

James Clemenson, War years, World War II.

James Clemenson and buddy in France, World War II.

Two navy boys, Guy and Lee Hart, World War II.

Gustav and Mavis Clemenson the War years, 1945.

GRANDMOTHER'S STORIES

WORLD WAR II

On December 7, 1941, Pearl Harbor was attacked. A sneak assault by the Japanese, destroyed our ships and carriers, our planes and hangars, and killed thousands of our service men. Our navy was seriously crippled. Our country writhed in horror and fear. How well I remember the next morning. Housewives gathered in groups on the sidewalk, talking excitedly, weeping and crying. Talking about husbands, brothers and sons who would be called away. War and the horror of war was fast approaching. President Roosevelt declared war on Japan. We would now fight on two fronts. We were all involved. I began attending first aid classes. A neighborhood Home Nursing Class was organized. Aunt Betty and I spent our evenings knitting sweaters for Bundles For Britain and discussing Hitler and his savagely brutal attack on the Jews.

We learned a whole new method of cooking. Sugar, coffee, meat and butter were all rationed. The choice cuts of beef and pork were sent to our boys on the front. Turkeys and chickens vanished on the same route. Kidneys, brains, tongues, liver, oxtails and sweet breads were left to us. I do remember saving up food stamps and getting a little pork sausage. Recipes were issued for cooking these glandular meats. The kidneys were supposed to soak in salt water overnight. They then could be boiled or baked. I never was able to mask the urine flavor, and we gave them up. We eliminated the fried brains and the boiled sweet breads, too. We liked fried liver. We learned to eat stuffed, baked heart, boiled tongue and oxtail soup became a great favorite.

Food stamps were issued and sugar was high in stamp value. We never had enough. I learned to make tasty jam with orange gum drops and rhubard. I baked our bread and rolls. We raised a garden. We ate well. Gas was rationed too. We went without a car for the duration. Gerhart walked to work and I was within walking distance to the grocery store.

A chill came over us as we saw brothers and cousins being drafted. We wondered when Gerhart's turn would come. We did not have long to wait. Almost immediately LaPlant Choate took over a government contract to build hydraulic equipment for trucks and tanks for the fighting front. Gerhart was made a night foreman and was frozen on the job. This meant that he would be there for the duration. We settled down to the grind of twelve or fourteen hours of working nights and sleeping days. The duration meant until the end of the war, and no one knew the length or the outcome. We could only endure and hope to survive. What would happen to all of us if Hitler succeeded in conquering the world as he vowed he would. He was coming dangerously close to his goal.

Gunder and Millie Clemenson from Kensett, Iowa, stopped for an overnight visit in March. They were on their way to California. Gunder had been drafted into the Navy and would begin boot training.

Gerhart's brother Jim was drafted and served as a medic in the Army. He was sent to Africa and went on to fight in Sicily, Italy and France. He was with Patton's 3rd Army and took part in the wipe-up of Germany. He saw many buddies shot down beside him. Jim was never counted among the sick or wounded. He made a promise to God that if he came home alive he would take care of his elderly parents as long as they lived. God spared him and Jim lived to go home and fulfill his promise.

Gus, another brother of Gerhart's, went into the Army. He was given a stateside desk job. My brother Vern received a farm deferment. He lived on a small farm in Minnesota and was sole support of his mother and brother George. My sister Elsie became a welder in the shipyards in Seattle. She helped repair the ghost ships which were being towed in from the South Pacific. My cousins Lee and Guy joined the Navy. Before the war was over, Lee had two ships sunk under him and was twice hospitalized for severe burns. Crystal went to Washington D.C. and took a desk job. Each week she donated one night of her time at the service men's center, visiting and counseling our homesick and frightened boys. Here is where she met Chuck Murphy, a handsome young man in the Marine Air Force. They married and Chuck flew away. He was a navigator bombardier, navigating his planes over towns and cities, releasing bombs.

We began to trust Uncle Sam and his mail service. Letters began to replace personal visits. They flew to the islands of the South Pacific, to Africa, Sicily, Italy and England. Letters from home were an important factor in maintaining the morale of the fighting front. Today our postal system is the most relaible of any postal service in the world.

Frozen on the job for the duration did not mean that Gerhart did not fulfill his part in the war effort. He worked long hard hours. First as a mechanic and later as a foreman. Right at the start he began to have trouble with the union. The union maintained that the company, LaPlant Choate, was making too much money. A work slow-up was ordered. This resulted in a decrease of the production of hydraulic pumps for the tanks and trucks on the fighting front. Gerhart and his Uncle Clemmy were stongly opposed to this practice. They took a strong stand. Gerhart told the union officials that he had a brother fighting this war and he would not consider a slow-up in his work. He and his uncle did all they could to encourage

GRANDMOTHER'S STORIES

high quality, maximum out-put. As a result of this Uncle Clemmy's machine was painted yellow. Gerhart was getting static of another form. He handled this in his characteristic manner by throwing one of the union officials out the window. Later several troublemakers challenged Gerhart to fight on the grounds outside the building. This did not materialize as the antagonists failed to show up. Gerhart was there though, eagerly waiting for them.

It was also at this time that we received a letter from the union telling us exactly who to vote for in the upcoming election, and informing us that we would be watched. A threat was thrown in as a scare tactic. We were angry at this procedure. Isn't it still a free country? Gerhart informed them that he would vote for whom he pleased. We would take no orders from the union.

By the spring of 1945 the war in Europe was over. Jim, who had served in Africa, Sicily and Italy and had fought through France to Belgian Bulge, and on into the wipe-up of Germany, was now home. He had served four years as a medic and came home unharmed. Gus was discharged. Our cousins drifted back from the Navy. All had stories to tell of ships sunk under them and buddies shot down beside them. Some carried scars of burns and shell-fire. All were home safe, and soon found their old places among friends and family. Jim bought the Gonvick Hotel. He served meals and rented rooms. His mother took over the kitchen and became head cook. He was able to fulfill his promise to God to take care of his parents as long as they lived. Gerhart left LaPlant Choate and went into police work. Leighton Ford, a friend of ours who had just received his discharge from the Army had returned from Germany and became Chief of Police of Marion. He began organizing the force. Gerhart was the first man hired, and from then on was privileged to wear the Number One badge. Two other men were hired. For some time Leighton, Gerhart, Dick Caylor and Walt Raunch made up the police force of the little city of Marion.

Officer Gerhart Clemenson, Marion Police Force, Marion, Iowa.

GRACE CLEMENSON

OUR HOME ON 18TH STREET

At the time Gerhart joined the police force we were living in Cedar Rapids. It became necessary for us to move to Marion. Marion was at that time a small town of less than ten thousand. Gerhart began working long hours again. He worked weekends with one Sunday off every other week.

It became my job to do the house hunting. We had a little home to sell. The dual situation became a challenge to the real estate men in both Cedar Rapids and Marion. They came down on me like a pack of wolves ready for a kill. They tried to sell me anything and everything no one else would want. They kept me running to look at termite infested hovels and rat ridden shacks. I began to distrust their word and I discovered many false statements and misrepresentations in their conversation. I wasn't interested in a house eaten up with termites. This seemed to be all they had to offer. I turned them all down. One day an agent came to show me one of his houses. I said, "No, I will not go with you any more. You are wasting my time." He said, "Mrs. Clemenson, don't you have to move?" I said, "I don't have to do anything." He turned to his partner and said, "We might as well leave. We can't do anything with her." This was the last I saw of them. A year went by. We still did not have a home in Marion. The Mayor was beginning to get perturbed with our delay. He sent word to me saying it was time to get settled in Marion. I sent word back to him saying that if we could find a suitable home we would gladly move. School was about to begin. I was getting uneasy.

One afternoon the doorbell rang and there stood another man with another house to sell. I was learning to say "NO!" and I said it. I told him that I was tired of looking at the kind of houses I had been shown. "They are all alike," I said, "rat infested and termite eaten." I would like to know who you people think we are." He was a very nice young man, one whom I had not seen before. He looked earnest and honest and said to me, "Tell me just what you are looking for." I stepped out onto the front porch where he was standing. I said, "See this clean well-kept neighborhood and this cozy home we are living in now? This is what I want. If there aren't any homes like this in Marion, I will stay here. And furthermore, I have to have a house near the bus line, near a school and near the shopping center and the library. I want a house that is well-built and can be lived in. And no termites or rats. Furthermore, we can't afford to pay any amount over ten thousand dollars. If you don't have anything with these quilifications, don't come back. He winked at me and said, "I will be back to get you in half an hour." I thought to myself, "I will never see him again." A half hour later the doorbell rang and there he stood. "I have found your house," he said. "Put on your hat and take the baby and come with me."

In the elite part of town stood a house - an old fashioned home which had been built in 1875. It was an eight-room house with nine-foot ceilings. The first thing I saw was a huge ell shaped front porch and a huge picture window. We walked into a vestibule which led into the reception room. This room had five long, narrow windows with venetian blinds. Underneath was a long window seat. French doors opened into a huge family room. This room was fourteen feet wide and sixteen feet long and had two beautiful large picture windows. From this room I walked back into the reception room and into a spacious dining room. The kitchen was huge and had two large windows facing South and two large windows facing West. We explored the basement. I found a coal furnace, a room for washing and lines for drying clothes. Upstairs were three bedrooms and a bath and an efficiency apartment. The hardwood floors were freshly varnished. The woodwork was newly painted and fresh new wallpaper dressed the walls. I liked what I saw. It was neat and clean. The location was just what I had ordered. I found the price was right for us—eight thousand dollars. I called Gerhart to come and look. He, too, was pleased, and that evening we closed the deal. The sale of our little home made the down payment on the larger home. In September of 1950 we moved again. We lived in this beautiful, spacious house until February of 1974. This was our home for twenty four years.

John was born here and the children all grew up here. They scattered their toys over the living room rug, boxed with their boxing gloves, roller skated in the halls and had pillow fights in the bedrooms. JoAnn and John played house on the stairway and camped out on the front porch. They built snowmen in the back yard and took fast sled rides on the front lawn. On hot summer nights they carried mattresses outdoors and slept under the stars. Birthdays were honored with parties and our Christmas parties were an annual event. We enjoyed our house, and it was well lived in.

John and Boots.

John and JoAnn.

GRACE CLEMENSON

The Gerhart Clemenson Family; Gerhart, JoAnn, Mavis, Grace, Vern, John, Gary, Christmas, 1965.

Our Home on 18th Street, Marion, Iowa, 1972. Kim Clemenson on porch.

GRANDMOTHER'S STORIES

MOTHER'S DEATH

On Memorial Day of 1947 my mother died suddenly of a heart attack. She had been sick a long time with gall bladder and heart trouble. Mother was fifty-five years old when she died. We had a car by this time and we drove to Gonvick, Minnesota, to her funeral. The funeral service was held for her in the Samhold Church of Gonvick. A second service was held in the Methodist Church in Grove Lake, Minnesota. Mother was raised in the Grove Lake community and this was her home church. She was buried in the cemetery where her parents, grandparents, aunts, uncles and cousins were buried. When I was a child I often heard my mother play the old hymn, "Going Down the Valley One by One." This hymn was sung again at mother's funeral. She was buried underneath the arms of a large oak tree. It was a sorrowful time, and difficult saying goodbye to a mother who had been so near and dear to me, one who had suffered so much pain and heartache and who had been a loving mother.

My father came to the funeral. We had not seen him for many years. Dad was born on May 11, 1882. When he died in March of 1963 we buried him beside mother. They are there together, lying side by side underneath an old oak tree in the Grove Lake cemetery. They are waiting the glorious morning when we shall be called up together to meet our Saviour in the air,

As I wrote these verses I thought of my mother's maternal ancestry, dating back to 1790 and residing in the mountains of Tennessee. The mountains, the mountain brooks and the mockingbird became part of my heritage.

"THE WOOING OF GOD'S SPIRIT"

The thunder on the mountain,
The sighing of the pines,
The babble of the pasture brook,
Speaks God's love divine.

There's an echo in the valley,
And a whispering in the trees,
A whipoorwill's soft calling,
Speaks God's love for me.

GRACE CLEMENSON

The lapping and the rippling,
Of a quiet water fall,
The mockingbird's soft trilling,
Sings out God's love to all.

The organ played at twilight,
My Mother sang to me,
In the softness of the evening,
She taught God's love to me.

God tunes my heart to listen,
Through the stillness of my soul,
to the wooing of His Spirit,
Guide me to a higher goal.

Mother's grave; Champ Maynard, Vern Maynard, Laura Halvorson, Buel Maynard, 1947.

Mother's funeral; Elsie Hallin, George Henry Johnston, Grace Clemenson, George Otis Johnston, Vern Johnston, Crystal Murphy, 1947.

Grove Lake Church, taken in 1963.

GRANDMOTHER'S STORIES

CHURCH AFFILIATIONS

Gerhart was a baptized and confirmed member of the Norwegian Lutheran Church at Gonvick, Minnesota. When we moved to Cedar Rapids we began attending the American Lutheran Church. As our family grew we became preoccupied and drifted away. For several years we had no religious interests. I felt lost and alone with no church home. One day I received a card in the mail and an invitation to sign up for a free Bible correspondence course. This is what I had been longing for. I signed the card and mailed it back. Soon I received my lessons and began my studies. I had not gone far when I was introduced to the Scriptural Sabbath. The Scriptural Sabbath is described in the first chapter of Genesis and is clearly stated in the Commandments given in the twentieth chapter of Exodus. It is the seventh-day Sabbath and requires us to rest and worship on the seventh day of the week, Saturday. This I believed and began to put into practice. This, too, turned my life completely around.

One day I received a phone call from a lovely lady who asked me if I would like to have some help with my lessons. I told her that I would like this. She came to see me and we had a few studies together. Then she invited me to attend her church with her on Saturday. I was happy with the idea and this was my introduction to the Seventh-Day Adventist Church. Mrs. White and I continued studying together. In these studies we covered the state of the dead, baptism by immersion, the meaning of tithing, and Jesus' Second Coming. We studied the book of Daniel, the golden image and Daniel's dreams. We studied the book of Revelation and the Third Angels' Messages. We continued studying on for two years. I prayed for God's guidance and felt the Holy Spirit with me. One evening I was talking to God in prayer and asking Him to show me what to pray for. Suddenly I saw words passing before my eyes spelling out a sentence. God was giving me my answer. His message to me was, "Give me the wisdom to know what is right. Give me the courage to do what is right." I knew then that God wanted me to pray for wisdom and courage. In my new-found religion I would need both. I was baptized soon after we made our move to Marion. Gary and Vern were attending Sunday School at the Presbyterian Church near us in Marion. I sent them off to Sunday School every Sunday, but on Saturday I took JoAnn and went to the Adeventist Church. One Sunday Gary said to me, "Mother, why do we have to go to church on Sunday? Why can't Vern and I go with you?" I was glad to hear this. I wanted them to make up their own minds. From that time on the children, Gary, Vern, JoAnn and I all went to church on Saturday.

During this time Gerhart was getting deeply involved with a life of his own. He had taken up poker playing. He worked long hours on the police force during the week. On weekends he met with his buddies around the poker table. We saw little of our father and husband. A year went by before he noticed there was something unusual going on in his home. One morning he looked at me rather curiously and said, "Grace, you are changed somehow. You seem happier, and you don't get angry at everything I say." I said, "Well, you see, I am converted now. I have been baptized into a new church. Haven't you noticed that the children and I board the bus and go somewhere every Saturday morning?" "Where do you go every Saturday morning?" he asked. "We go to Cedar Rapids, back to our old neighborhood where there is a Seventh-Day Adventist Church," I answered. "You can stop that right now. I won't have you going there," he said. It was too late for changes now. Gerhart went back to his poker friends and we kept going to church. We had been adopted into a new family, a loving church family which was just what we needed. And loving they were. They gave us the spiritual nourishment we were hungering for and the social life we were in need of.

Sabbath was a day we looked forward to and prepared for all through the week. Every day we repeated our memory verses and learned them for the coming Sabbath. On Friday I did the baking and cooking. We polished shoes, took baths and laid out our clothes. At sundown we were ready for stories, songs, prayers and early to bed. Often on Sabbath morning we packed a lunch and prepared to stay at church all day. Gary and Vern sang in the children's choir and took part in the Missionary Volunteer meetings. JoAnn and her girlfriend Norma Jean Evans, sang together for church and afternoon programs. One Sabbath afternoon Gary was asked to give a book review of one of the children's books from the church library. The book was about a snake in the schoolroom. It got into the teacher's desk. Gary finished by saying, "If you want to know what happened to the teacher, read the book." Saturday night was party night. We were often invited to various homes for an evening of games and visiting. Apples, popcorn and grape juice were standard refreshments. Our spacious living room was the center of many Saturday night get-togethers. In the winter we had sledding parties, in the summer camping trips, picnics and swimming.

Then there was camp meeting—a happy, joyous occasion, held for a week at the Academy at Nevada, Iowa. Many families planned their vacations then and took their tents and children and stayed for the week. We were happy to be able to go for a weekend. I rememeber so well the time we went to camp meeting with Dorothy Millburn, Connie, Doug and Dennie. Dorothy had a small car, but she knew just how to load it to make the best use of every corner. Suitcases were tied on top. Pots, pans and dishes and foodstuffs went into the trunk. Gary, Vern, JoAnn, Connie, Doug and Dennie were stuffed in the back seat with pillows and towels and extra bedding. Dorothy drove and I sat beside her with a cooler under my feet and a cake on my lap. We looked like a band of gypsies taking to the road.

We left on Friday afternoon. We hoped to have plenty of time to get our tents set up before sundown. The day was hot and humid as summer afternoons are in Iowa. For air-conditioning we rolled down all the windows. All went well until we got out of town. Then suddenly with a jerk and a sigh the old car stopped. We all got out to look under the hood. Joggling and juggling of wires did no good. Dorothy checked out the basics, oil, water and gas. There was no shortage there. We stood around wondering what to do next. The Lord knew the answer to our problem and sent help even before we asked. As we walked around feeling perplexed and helpless, a car stopped. It was our pastor and his family on the way to camp meeting. Pastor Gregerhof got our car started and took part of our load. Gary, Vern and Doug changed cars and drove off ahead of us. Dorothy and the remainder of her load drove on to Nevada with no further trouble. We set up our tents and ate our supper. We were all on time for the Friday night meeting.

Gerhart found our new faith very hard to accept. He was very much opposed to our church activities and our comings and goings. One Sabbath morning we woke up to the sound of rain pounding at our windows. I got up and prepared our breakfast. We were eating when Gerhart, who had been at work on the night shift, came in. He stood by the kitchen door shedding little pellets of raindrops. "Well," he said, "you won't go to church today. It is raining out there." "Oh, yes, we will," I said, "for when we get ready to go out that door it will stop raining." Gerhart walked through the kitchen and upstairs to his room. Gary looked at me and said, "What shall we do now, Mother?" I said, "Let's pray about it." After prayer, Gary said, "What shall we do now, Mother?" I said, "Let's get ready to go." We dressed for church and the rain kept coming down. We didn't own a raincoat, boots or umbrella. We had a half block to go to catch the bus. We walked out onto the front porch to look at the rain, when suddenly it stopped. We looked around amazed and walked off the porch. We looked up into the sky, but there was still no rain. We walked to the bus stop, boarded the bus and went to church. We rode the bus home after church and still no rain. We went into the house and hurried to change clothes and eat our lunch. While we were sitting at the table our attention was drawn to a pounding on the windows. We were surprised to see the rain coming down in torrents, just as it had at the breakfast table. We all got the message. God had answered another prayer.

Several weeks later we again awoke on a Sabbath morning to the sound of rain on our roof. Gerhart came home while we were eating breakfast. He shook off the raindrops, looked at us and said, "Well, you won't get to church today. It's raining out there." Gary spoke up and said, 'Oh, yes we will, Daddy, because when we get ready to go out the door it will stop raining." We said a prayer, dressed again in our Sabbath best. We walked out onto the porch and the rain stopped. We caught the bus and got to church on another rainy day. When we got home, the rain again took up its pounding and sloshing on our windows and porches. It continued to rain all afternoon and night and all day Sunday. The Lord knew our needs and heard our prayer. How well he provided for us.

Amos 4:7 tells us, "And also I have witholden the rain from you."

One of my favorite memories of the Cedar Rapids Seventh Day Adventist Church was my six years as Pathfinder Leader. We had between fifteen and twenty boys and girls. John Clemenson. Donita Blisa and Vernon Mathis were little Pre-Pathfinders for two years of that time.

We were an active group. Camping was our favorite summer activity. We learned to pitch tents and dig latrines, to build fires and cook over them. We learned the birds, flowers and edible plants of the area.

We worked on honors and earned badges in leather craft, poster making, sewing, cooking, Indian lore, swimming, camping, first aid and many others. One of our counselors had experience as drill master in the army. He drilled us with a vengence. We learned formation marching with right face, left face and about face. In this we won the state honors at the Pathfinder fair one year.

One of my favorite times was our Wilderness Survival Camp Out. We chose a remote site on an island, the property of one of our members. We spent one Friday afternoon transporting campers, tents and camping gear in a row boat, up-stream and across the Wapsi River to our campsite. There we quickly pitched tents, built fires and cooked our evening meal.

Our Friday night sundown service was held around a huge bon fire. After the last song was sung the tired campers rolled into their sleeping bags exhausted.

Our Sabbath activities consisted of Sabbath School and Church under the trees near a rippling stream. The afternoon was spent in a nature treasure hunt, nature walk and an afternoon service with Bible games and singing.

On Sunday we spent the morning building shelters from branches and vines, hunting and cooking wild herbs and roots and making Sumac Tea. In the afternoon we learned to make smoke signals. We practiced First Aid. After a quick evening meal we packed up, loaded our boat and began our trip home.

After six years I was exhausted. I turned the leadership over to another ambitious soul. During this time I had earned my Master Guide honor. I was invested at a Candle Light Service in Minneapolis, Minnesota. A hundred or so of us all carried lighted candles. A beautiful service and happy ending to my six years as Pathfinder Leader.

Pathfinder Boys, Cedar Rapids, Iowa, 1959.

Pathfinder Girls, Cedar Rapids, Iowa, 1961.

Pathfinder Girls, Cedar Rapids, Iowa, 1959.

Pre-Pathfinder, John Clemenson, 1962.

Pathfinder Fair, Des Moines, Iowa, 1961.

Pre-Pathfinders, Vernon Mathis, John Clemenson, 1961.

GRANDMOTHER'S STORIES

OUR CAMPING TRIPS

Gerhart worked steady on the police force. He did some moonlighting, driving truck for Henry Katz. He kept himself busy night and day. Even on Sunday he would find a fire to chase or some convict from the Anamosa Penitentiary to hunt down.

I felt a need for some activity to create more family togetherness. Our friends, Perry and Sherma Wells, introduced us to the primitive style of camping. At that time we had no tents, no sleeping bags, no stove, and no lantern. "Never mind that," said Perry and Sherma, "we camp like this all the time. We build a fire inside a circle of rocks."

This served us for warmth and cooking. We took food that would cook well on the coals. We liked pancakes with syrup and eggs for breakfast. For lunch we toasted sandwiches and heated a pot of soup. Potatoes and corn cooked crisp and tasty in a bed of hot coals, and beans baked in the hot ashes served us for our suppers. After supper and clean-up Gerhart would cut long marshmallow sticks from tree branches. We ate toasted marshmallows for dessert. It was hard to give up and go to bed. We sat around the dying embers and sang the old camp songs. "Good Night, Ladies," was the signal for bed. As we lay on our mats around the fire we watched the stars and the rising moon while we waited for sleep. How well I remember the time we were awakened by a scuffing sound. A little animal was busy dragging off one of John's little shoes. Another time one of JoAnn's anklets came up missing. One night we saw the eyes of a deer watching us from a safe distance.

We camped this way for a couple of summers. Then Gerhart picked up a second-hand tent. Gary and Vern bought tents of their own. Camping became more comfortable. We pitched under a shady tree near the Wapsipinicon River. With our axes we chopped down the brush around us, with shovels we dug trenches around the tents. The tents were not strong enough to withstand the severe outbursts of Iowa thunder storms. They flapped and shook as the wind blew the rain under us and upon us. Morning found us hanging our bedding on a limb and building a fire with wet wood.

We enjoyed the out-of-doors, the wild flowers, the blue sky, the lazy river. In the evening the fireflies lighted up the darkness and the stars twinkled high above the tree tops.

We camped this way until JoAnn and Mavis were teenagers, and Gary had left for the navy. One day Gerhart bought an Iowa City bus. We all went to work remodeling. Gerhart hired carpenters to build bunks, a table and chest of drawers. JoAnn, Mavis, and John all helped with the painting. I kept busy making curtains. Soon we began camping in style in our very own camper bus. It was equipped with a stove, refrigerator, cupboards, drawers, bunks, a table, and four stools.

Now we widened our camping range. For several summers we traveled and camped in the state parks around the county. The Wapsipenican State Park was our favorite and most frequented spot. The Wapsi River had the best swimming holes. There were no lakes in our area. The children learned to swim in the American Legion pool in Marion. They were all good swimmers. JoAnn completed the course in Adult Life Saving. On these outings we had to consider the advantages of swimming. Several times we went to McGregor, Iowa, on the Mississippi River. We met Crystal and Chuck there on two occasions. Kit, at this time, was learning to play the guitar. How well I remember the fun times we had singing along together with the guitar for accompaniment.

One day the old bus wore out. Repairs were impossible. Parts were obselete. This put and end to our wanderings on the bus as we settled in a permanent home. John Brunen, a friend of Gerhart's, leased us a little chunk of land on the Cedar River. This is where we parked our camper bus. This was a beautiful spot to settle down on. In May several cherry trees on a corner of the lot came into full bloom. Their beauty and fragrance were unsurpassed. In the autumn, red and yellow oak leaves carpeted our lawn. Gooseberries and blackberries were plentiful all summer. In the spring and fall we went mushroom hunting.

With a bird book and binoculars, Gerhart and I became bird watchers. We watched a family of Jenny Wrens build a nest on a near-by fence post. Our lawn became a nursery for baby robins just learning to fly. We watched the Baltimore orioles build their basket nests, and listened to the sweet, musical songs of the meadowlark. How well I remember one early evening in summer. Gerhart and I went to bed at sundown. As we lay awake looking out at the sunset, a bob o'link stopped under our window. He sat there and sang his song of bobo'link, bobo'link, bobo'link for a full five minutes. We listened in perfect rapture for we felt he was singing just for us. We enjoyed this camp sight for several summers. We moved to Spokane in the spring of 1974, and willed the camper to Gary and Sharon.

Iowa is situated in the center of a tornado belt. June is considered to be tornado month. Cities, small towns and farms are victims of the whirling winds. The sight of a funnel-shaped cloud brings fear and dread to the hearts of many. It often means complete destruction of homes and loss of life. The violent winds sweep a path of demolition and ruin for miles across the country.

How well I remember the tornado that hit Marion in the spring of 1965. Gary was home from the service, having served four years in the navy. He and John were sleeping in the boy's room. JoAnn was asleep in her room across the hall from me. At three o'clock in the morning I was awakened to hear Gary shouting, "Head for the basement." I sprang out of bed, ran into JoAnn's room to wake her. I saw pictures, books and papers twirling around the room. I felt the old house rock. We ran for the basement. In a minute it was all over.

We gathered on the front porch to view the damage. Fallen trees, branches and electric wires were tangled together. A tree had fallen on the roof of the house across the street. The neighbor, Laura Badham, was standing on her porch crying and shouting. She wanted Gerhart to come and take the tree off her roof. Gerhart was on police duty and was involved in his own troubles, and because of the entanglement of trees and wires on our street he was unable to get home. Some time in the afternoon the power company line men reached us and began their work of cutting branches and replacing wires. We lost several beautiful American Elm trees. No damage was done to our home on 18th Street. Buildings and homes in other parts of town were dismantled. JoAnn and I put pictures, books, lamps and curtains back in place in her room. We were all very thankful for having escaped, so well, the vicious blows of Mother Nature.

A neighbor of ours had a brother living on a nearby farm who did not fare as well. As he was herding his family into the storm cellar the kitchen door flew past and cut off his ear. Many stories and unusual happenings have been told resulting from these wild rages of nature. Farm animals have been lifted up and carried through the air and set down in fields many miles from home. I once read of the kitchen doors being torn off homes and carried away. Then the refrigerator, stove and table sucked out the door one by one and up into the funnel. The family watching in horror were left untouched.

Tornadoes are fearful whirling winds accompanied by torrents of rain, zig zags of lightning and bellows of thunder; cutting a narrow path of destruction for many miles across the land.

GRACE CLEMENSON

Christmas, 1950.

Gerhart Clemenson, Verl Lindberg, Christmas 1973.

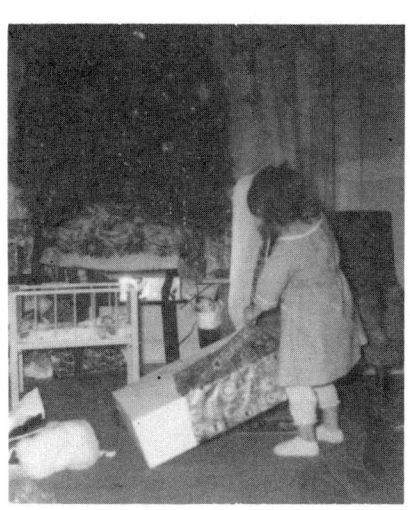

Michelle Newhard, Christmas, 1972.

Kimberly, Sharon and John Clemenson, Christmas, 1968.

GRANDMOTHER'S STORIES

CHRISTMAS AT 960-18th STREET

Christmas was a galla time in the old house. Our Christmas tree was huge and tall, the top being securely fastened to the nine-foot ceiling. Gary, Vern, and JoAnn began work early in December, making gifts and home-made ornaments. Red and green paper chains, stars, bells, and strings of popcorn decorated the branches. At the top sat a pink feather angel, a gift frm Mrs. Stuber to JoAnn. On Christmas Eve the packages were stacked under the tree, proudly displaying their bows and ribbons.

Our Christmas Eve supper was traditionally Norwegian. When Gerhart was a boy at home, his mother served his lutifisk with melted butter, lefsa and boiled potatoes. To this I added a salad, homemade rolls, and fruit cake. After our supper in the dining room, we left the table and went into the living room. The tree lights were turned on and the rush began. Paper and ribbons flew as gifts were opened. What joy! What delight! A homemade doll for JoAnn, as well as a doll bed and stool, each painted red, built from apple boxes by Gary and Vern. Sweaters, mittens, caps and slippers all popped out of their wrappers. Susie, our cocker spaniel, received her bone wrapped in Christmas tissue and tied with a ribbon bow. She could dismantle it as quickly as any child. Soon the gifts were all opened and the children settled down to play. I cleared the table and washed up the dishes. Gerhart picked up papers and burned the trash. We were then ready for our sight-seeing trip, to Cedar Rapids to view the Christmas lights.

We lived in the small town of Marion, and our drive to Cedar Rapids was a delight. We watched for manger scenes, Santas with reindeer on roof tops, and brightly decorated shrubs and trees. Prizes were given to the most beautifully decorated homes. We joined the long parade of cars cruising up and down the streets on Christmas Eve. Midnight was our bed time. We found it hard to settle down. Stockings were hung, and milk and cookies set out for old Santa. The goodnights were said. Still little ears listened and eyes would not close.

Gerhart and I began our work. Stockings were filled as quietly as possible. An orange went into the toe of everyone's stocking. Nuts and candy followed, perhaps then a little box of trinkets, a little doll, and a knife or whistle, until the stocking could hold no more. Sleds, dolls, books, and clothing we piled around the tree. Santa's work was done, and his two helpers fell into bed exhausted. We were awakened on Christmas morning by shouts of joy. Santa had indeed come. Only a few crumbs of a cookie were found left on the table, and he drank all of his milk.

GRACE CLEMENSON

Now it is time to prepare for the annual Clemenson Christmas party. Gerhart's aunts, uncles, sisters, brothers, nieces, and nephews gathered for an afternoon and evening of visiting, eating, and the lighting of the tree. For this party we drew names for a gift exchange, and everyone brought a contribution to the Christmas dinner. As many as twenty relatives could sometimes be expected, and especially so in the later years when our families began to grow. But no matter, there was plenty of room in the big old house.

The dining room was huge, and the table with the leaves adjusted could seat everyone comfortably. A huge turkey was set at one end of the table, and Gerhart and his brother-in-law Verl struggled with the carving. Plates were passed for light and dark meat according to everyone's taste. Potatoes, gravy, dressing, cranberries, vegetables, rolls, and lefsa were passed around. Pie and coffee would be served later in the evening. When dinner was over, Aunt Betty, Ellen, and I helped with the kitchen clean-up. We cleared the table, put away food, and washed dishes while the children played with their new games and the men folks visited.

Now we were ready for the tree. One Christmas Uncle Ed played Santa Claus. I helped him make a suit of a red hunting jacket and pants. I trimmed it with white cotton batting. I made a red cap and white beard. On the night of the party I took all of the exchange gifts and put them into Santa's bag. I set the bag in the garage. After dinner Uncled Ed slipped out the back door and into the garage to dress. Soon he came up on the front porch and jingled his sleigh bells. The children's ears tingled and eyes popped open. I opened the door and exclaimed, "Why, Santa Claus, we weren't expecting you so soon! Come in! Come in!" Santa stepped in, nodded his head and opened his bag. He had a gift for everyone.

John was two years old, and the youngest of the group. Santa told him that he had something special for him out in his sleigh. As John waited, Santa came in with a bright yellow riding tractor. John sat down on the tractor and looked up at Santa. Suddenly he exclaimed, "Oh, look, Mother! Santa Claus is wearing Uncle Ed's boots!"

Santa shouted, "Merry Christmas to all!" and slipped out the door. Christmas was over for another year.

GRANDMOTHER'S STORIES

GARY'S STORY

Gary graduated from the Marion High School in nineteen sixty. He was tired of school and had no interest in college. One day he decided he would join the Navy. He and his friend made plans to join together. They talked to the Navy recruiter and the date was set. I objected. I told Gary that my fears were that he would take up drinking. Our young boys away from home for the first time in the services were heavily exposed to alcohol. Many came home with drinking problems. Gary related my fears to the recruiting agent. The recruiter was concerned and he came to talk to me. I told him I did not want Gary to go into the Navy. I was angry at the way the beer barrels were rolled out and the alcohol consumed in the services. The recruiter did not convince me that all would be well. He did have a talk with Gary. Gary had a good Navy hitch, and he came home sober.

After finishing Navy school, Gary was assigned to the aircraft carrier WASP and went to sea. His first appointment was with the NATO tour. This was a goodwill tour which took him into England, Holland, Germany, Norway, Iceland, and across the Arctic Circle. On the Caribbean cruise he visited the islands of Cuba, Haiti, Jamaica, and Puerto Rico. These were called Goodwill Tours. They were launched to promote goodwill between our country and the countries they were visiting. The boys helped repair public buildings and homes that were torn up during the war. They passed out food and clothing parcels to the needy. They held open house on the ship and enjoyed many sight-seeing trips. "Join the Navy and see the world" proved true for Gary.

During his four years in the Navy, Gary corresponded with Sharon Wood, a home town girl and friend of the family. Now that he was home again, they continued their courtship and were married on November 3, 1966. One morning upon arising early, I walked into the kitchen and found this note on the kitchen table.

> *"Good Morning, everyone! Boy, I still haven't figured out what we are doing up at this wee hour of the night. Well, now down to business. Just thought we'd let you know we have eloped. Will be home in two or so days.*
>
> *Love,*
> *Sharon and Gary*

Lois and I planned a reception. Gifts began coming in. When Gary and Sharon

GRACE CLEMENSON

arrived home three days later, family and friends gathered together at the Wood home to welcome them.

Their first home was a mobile home in a trailer court near us. Gary began working for the Bell Telephone Company. Soon they announced that a baby was on the way. Kimberly Sue was our first grandchild. She was a bright blue-eyed baby with blond hair and rosy cheeks. She came to visit us often. How well I remember her little feet pattering up the sidewalk to our house, running and calling, "I's coming, Grandma. I's coming." She loved to stay overnight. Quite often she stayed for a weekend. I prepared a special room for her with a crib and rocking chair. Brenda and Michelle shared this room together as they came along.

Brenda Ann was our fourth grandchild. Brenda was tall and lanky and possessed a great deal of courage and stamina. I remember her walking four miles from her home in the country to our home in the city when she was three years old. She came breezing into the kitchen with her mother, smiling and active and with no sign of fatigue. Brenda was always very active and never seemed to tire. She has grown to be six feet, two inches tall and is a star basketball player for the Amateur Athletic Association. She also plays basketball at Gonzaga Prep.

Gary is a Network Technician with North West Bell in Spokane, Washington.

Sharon and Gary Clemenson Married, Nov. 3, 1966.

Kimberly, Brenda, Sharon Clemenson.

GRANDMOTHER'S STORIES

VERN'S STORY

Vern was a healthy, happy six-year-old, always on the run, always ready to go, when he became suddenly ill.

He was in the first grade, and had been in school about four weeks. One day he came home crying. His knees ached. I saw that they were swollen and red. I saw also that he was running a low-grade temperature. He complained of being tired. I suspected something serious and called the doctor. The diagnosis was mononucleosis. The doctor told me to keep him home and in about three weeks' time it would run its course.

Vern was home and in and out of bed for two months. On his better days he sat at the kitchen table and worked on school assignments and workbooks. His better days grew less and less as he spent more time in bed. I called the doctor again and told him he would have to take some immediate action; Vern was no better. Finally, just before Christmas, Vern was hospitalized. Blood tests showed rheumatic fever. He began to receive proper medication and began a slow improvement.

Vern enjoyed his hospital stay. His daddy arranged a phone call for him from Santa Claus. One afternoon the phone rang at the desk and Santa asked to speak to Vern Clemenson. The nurses rushed to his room and brought him out in a wheel chair. Photographers were there from the Cedar Rapids Gazette. Gary, JoAnn, and I turned on the radio at home and heard Vern and Santa talking. "Hello, Vern. Merry Christmas! I am calling all the way from the North Pole. I am wondering what you would like to have me bring you for Christmas," Santa said. "I want a Tinker Toy set most of all," Vern replied, "and a sled and some candy if you have some." "Oh yes," said Santa. "I will put my little elves to work right away building the sled and making Tinker Toys. Mrs. Santa will make the candy. You be a good boy now and get well and get home for Christmas." Vern did get home for Christmas, and was able to go back to school in January. He continued to suffer from fatigue and continued to run a low-grade temperature for many months. He was an eighth-grader before he completely regained his health.

Vern, during his early teens, kept himself busy mowing lawns in summer. He was twelve years old when this story took place. He needed a new lawn mower. His dad said, "No." He could not buy a new one that summer. Vern went to Bryd's Hardware Store one morning and made a deal with Mr. Byrd. About ten o'clock that morning I looked out the kitchen window and saw Vern coming down the alley pushing a brand new lawn mower. "Vern," I said, "where did you get that lawn mower?" "Mr. Byrd let me have it," he said. "I told him I would pay for it with my mowing money." Henry Katz gave Vern his first job mowing a field. He paid Vern one dollar an hour for his mower and one dollar an hour for his time. Vern mowed lawns all summer and Mr. Byrd got paid for his mower. When Vern turned sixteen he sold his mower to John who took over his brother's business.

Gary was sixteen when he began working for Ralph Heckroth's gas station. One noon he came home for lunch, hungry, tired and discouraged. We were all quietly eating our meal when Gary suddenly announced that he was going to quit working for Ralph. It seemed that Gary had asked for a raise and go no response. No one commented on Gary's decision, but Vern, who was looking for a job, had his ears open and his brain working. The next morning before Gary went to work, Vern went to see Ralph. "When Gary quits, can I have his job?" he asked Ralph. Ralph was surprised. "Is Gary quitting?" he asked. "Yes," Vern answered, "he wants more money." Vern didn't get the job, but Gary got the raise.

Vern was sixteen when he went to work for Byrl Dicky at Dicky's gas station. This was an after school and weekend job. John followed Vern's footsteps and went to work for Bryl Dickey when he was fourteen. Byrl and John signed a child-labor law form agreeing on the maximum number of hours John would be allowed to work. It seemed that with John's eagerness to work he sometimes exceeded these hours. He pumped gas, changed tires, and operated the cash register. The boys liked Byrl; he was great to work for.

Vern graduated from the Marion High Shool in the spring of 1963. He continued working for Byrl at the gas station, saving his money for college. He received a loan from Walla Walla College at College Place, Washington. After two years of college he served two years in the Army. He attended officers' training school at Lawton, Oklahoma. He was assigned duties at Fort Lewis near Tacoma, Washington.

On July third of 1969 Vern and Judy Lillenthal were married in the Chapel of the Pacific Lutheran University in Tacoma, Washington. Vern insisted that Gerhart and I be present at the wedding. Arrangements were made for us to board the train in Minneapolis. We had a delightful ride in the executive coach on the Great Northern. We sat all day in the dome car watching the changes of scenery as we rolled westward. Wheat fields flew by, golden and glistening in the summer sun, stretching out as far as the eye could see. Acres of yellow sunflowers nodded to us along the way. Deer and antelope grazed beside the track until the whistle of the train sent them racing across the prairie. We were fascinated by the tumbled log cabins, broken corrals, and old wooden windmills left lonely and abandoned on the wind-swept prairies. The home on the range is gone. The buffalo roam no more.

GRANDMOTHER'S STORIES

God still guides the night, and the heavens are bright with the light from the glittering stars. These words from *Home on the Range* came to mind. Thank you, God, for the beauty of the heavens, the glory of the stars. Thank you for the comforts of your beautiful creation.

After the wedding, Vern and Judy left for their honeymoon. Gerhart and I made our return trip home on the Great Northern, traveling across the Great Plains and on to Minneapolis. This was a fabulous trip, a second honeymoon for us.

Scott, our first grandson, was born in Spokane. When I moved to Spokane and became widowed, Scott spent many weekends with me. He climbed my trees and fell out. He helped me plant a garden in the spring and we dug potatoes in the fall. When he got tired of me and wanted to go home he would say, "I have to go home now. I don't like the spiders in your house." Scott liked my milk toast though, and still eats milk toast for breakfast on occasion. Scott's early childhood hobby was collecting antiques. He and I liked to walk through the woods near his home and hunt for hidden treasures. Behind an abandoned chicken pen we found a board with a square nail, an old door with leather hinges, and broken bits of a buttercrock, all relics of bygone days.

Scott was in the first grade when his brother Travis was born. Travis was a bright, blue-eyed baby with red hair that shone like a pot of gold in the sunshine. Travis was four years old when he started an old bone collection. We took many long walks together, searching the woods for old bones. We carried home skulls, leg bones and rib bones. One day we found a perfect skeleton of a little mouse lying at the foot of a tree. This we thought was the most interesting find of all. We picked it up carefully and carried it home in a kleenex. Travis put it in a little box for safekeeping. God knows all about the little creatures of the forest. He says in His book, "Every beast of the field is mine. The cattle on a thousand hills. I know every bird of the mountain." Proverbs 50: 9, 10.

Scott and Travis have twin brothers, Connor and Tyler, born on February 5, 1984. They are healthy, happy babies. Soon I will be walking through the woods with them. I wonder what their hobbies will be. At this writing they are three years old. They come to visit me once a month. I take them to church and Sabbath school. When they go home they say to their mother, "We sit quiet in church." They are learning Bible stories and singing, "Jesus Loves Me." God's eye is on the sparrow. He watches over them.

Vern is now president of his own investment company. Investors Northwest: in Spokane, Washington.

GRACE CLEMENSON

Judy and Vern Clemenson
Married, July 3, 1969.

Travis Clemenson with his twin brothers, Connor and Tyler.

Scott Clemenson, the Fisherman.

Grace Clemenson and twins, Connor and Tyler.

GRANDMOTHER'S STORIES

JOANN'S STORY

Gary and Vern began hunting as soon as they were old enough to walk and carry a gun. Gerhart took them squirrel hunting in September, pheasant hunting in October, deer hunting in November. Fox hunting came in February and March. Uncle Clemmy was a member of the party, and together they made a happy foursome.

One afternoon Gerhart came home from his work at Katz Salvage. JoAnn and John coaxed their dad to take them hunting. They took the B-B gun and set out for the woods to look for squirrels. They came home after an hour and a half of hunting. Gerhart went to bed to rest before night duty on the police force. JoAnn and John went into the basement to target practice with the B-B gun.

Suddenly JoAnn came into the kitchen crying. Blood was streaming from her right eye. John followed her and told me what had happened. They were preparing to shoot at the target when a B-B caught in the barrel of the gun. JoAnn looked down the barrel and the gun suddenly went off. A B-B went through her eye. I washed her eye and put a wet washcloth on it. Now Gerhart was up and JoAnn and her dad raced for the hospital. I followed soon after.

When I arrived at the hospital I found JoAnn in a state of shock. Uncle Henry Katz had been there, too, and gave her a fifty-cent piece and told her to be a good girl. JoAnn clutched the fifty-cent piece tight in her hand, but did not feel like being a good girl. She refused to let the doctors examine her eye. She fought and cried. She complained that she had had no supper and she was hungry. The interns and nurses were running wildly around. A crowd was gathering in her room. Relatives came. Friends and neighbors heard of the accident and hurried to the hospital. All was bedlam. There was no one to take charge.

Finally a specialist arrived. He ordered that she be moved to an examining room. There she was put on a table and a bright light was turned on over her head. The crowd of people from the first room followed into the second and stood along the wall. The doctor explained to me the seriousness of the situation. He said he would have to take pictures to find where the B-B was lodged. "This may take all night," he said, "and I will need her complete cooperation." Then he added, "Mrs. Clemenson, we are not getting it." I said to him, "JoAnn understands about the power of prayer. I would like a good half-hour of quiet time to pray with her. But those people standing along the wall will have to leave. The bright light will have to be turned off." I took hold of JoAnn's hand and bowed my head in prayer.

I opened my eyes to see the people had vanished. The lights were turned low and the doctor was softly closing the door behind him. We were alone, JoAnn and I and the Holy Spirit. I already began to feel His presence with us. All was very quiet. JoAnn and I began to talk. She was a child who had been brought up with prayer. She closed her eyes as I held her hand and prayed. I asked God for the infilling of the Holy Spirit, for His healing hand in this emergency, for calm and peace and a cooperative spirit. I talked to JoAnn again. I told her that the doctor would come in and turn on the bright overhead light. He would have instruments to look into her eye. He would be giving her directions to follow and she must cooperate. "God will help you," I said. We prayed again, and a great peace came over us. The Holy Spirit filled the room. JoAnn fell asleep.

The doctor came in and found her still sleeping. I told him that she was ready and would now cooperate. She opened her eyes as the light went on. The doctor began his work. He took the first picture as JoAnn held her eye in a steady position. He went out to examine it. He came back very excited. "We found the B-B," he said, "and it is lodged in her forehead. It is in a place where it will do no harm. There will be no need for an operation." This was good news. I breathed a prayer of thanks.

A nurse came in with a wheel chair to take JoAnn to her room. It was nine o'clock and the doctor would do no more work on her eye that night. JoAnn reminded us that she had had no supper and she was hungry. I asked the intern in charge if she could have a lunch. He said, "Oh, no, Mrs. Clemenson. We don't serve food after hours." I said, "You are in charge here, aren't you?" He said, "Yes." I said, "Then you give the orders, don't you?" He said, "Yes." I said, "My daughter is hungry and you can order a meal for her if you want to, and you do it." When we got up to JoAnn's room a pretty little lunch was waiting for her at her bedside table. She slept well that night.

The next morning I went to the hospital and found JoAnn in bed with both eyes bandaged. An eye specialist had examined her eye. He gave us no hope for any sight from that eye. He said that the bandages must remain on for one full week. She must not cry. Tears would hinder the healing process. JoAnn always wanted to cry when I left her. We talked about the eye and the tears. She said she wouldn't cry when I left if I would promise to come back. We prayed that we would both be brave. JoAnn came home a week later on Thanksgiving Day.

We had another appointment with our doctor. JoAnn sat on a stool in front of the doctor and I sat in a chair behind him. After the eye test was completed, the doctor swiveled around in his swivel chair and faced me. "Mrs. Clemenson, I am astounded. JoAnn has perfect vision in both eyes," he exclaimed. "God is so good," I said, prayers have been answered.

JoAnn graduated from the Marion High School in May of nineteen hundred and sixty-five. During her junior and senior years she worked part time at Kendall's Hardware store. She coninued to work there through the summer after graduation. In the fall she began work at Cherry Barrell.

While JoAnn was working there, she met Truman Newhard. They dated several months and decided to get married. We began planning a November wedding.

JoAnn made a beautiful bride. She chose a gown of deluster satin which was fashioned in an Empire A-line style. The batteau neckline was trimmed with a double lace ruffle. The three-quarter length sleeves were trimmed with the same lace ruffle. Her head piece was a cluster of jeweled flowers. To this was attached a chapel-length train. In her hand JoAnn carried a bouquet of white roses with feathered mums and long ivy.

Gerhart gave his girl away. Mavis was maid of honor. Her gown was made of gold velvet, cut with a sweetheart neckline and was made up of gold roses and a shoulder length veil. Nancy Newhard and Sharon Clemenson were bridesmaids. Their gowns were identical to the gown Mavis wore. Susan Meyers was JoAnn's flower girl. Susan wore an empire-style gown with three-quarter length sleeves. The neckline and sleeves were accented with lace.

A reception for two hundred was held at the church parlor. The four-tier wedding cake was decorated with gold roses. After the gifts were opened, JoAnn and J.R. slipped away. JoAnn changed into a brown dress and coat ensemble with a corsage of fall pompoms. Now they were off on their honeymoon.

JoAnn became a full-time housewife. She and J.R. bought a home on the west side of Cedar Rapids. They began raising a garden and a family. Michelle Rene was born on July 21, 1970. She was a beautiful dark-haired dark-eyed baby, serious and intelligent. She and Kim and Brenda were frequent weekend visitors in our home.

How well I remember this little story of an incident that took place in our kitchen one afternoon. Kim, Brenda, Michelle and I were having lunch together. The door opened suddenly and Uncle Clemmy walked in. He sat down by the table, took a nickel out of his pocket, and gave it to Brenda. He took a quarter out of his pocket and gave it to Kim. Then he took out another nickel and gave it to Michelle. Because she was only two years old he thought she would not know the difference between a quarter and a nickel. Michelle looked at the nickel a minute, then she threw it across the room. "I don't want that old nickel," she cried. Uncle Clemmy found a quarter and held it up. "Do you want this?" he asked. Michelle took the quarter and looked at him searchingly as though to say, "Don't play tricks on me." Uncle Clemmy and I were very much amazed and had a good chuckle over this.

At this writing Michelle is living with me. She is sixteen years old and is attending the Spokane Junior Academy. She sings in the school choir, earns her pin money by baby-sitting, and is preparing to run in the Bloomsday race.

When Michelle was two years old, JoAnn and J.R. were divorced. JoAnn continued her education at the Kirkwood Community College in Cedar Rapids. She was working on an associate degree in nursing, when she was hospitalized with viral meningitis. She was still in the hospital when Gerhart and I moved to Spokane. We took Michelle and JoAnn's car and household goods with us. We planned to fly JoAnn to Spokane as soon as the doctor released her. Gerhart died suddenly three weeks after we arrived in Spokane. We took him back to Marion for a funeral service. JoAnn remarried soon after the funeral and continued to make her home in Iowa.

JoAnn is a housewife and home-maker and lives in Story City, Iowa.

**JoAnn and J.R. Newhard
Married, Nov., 1968**

Michelle Newhard, 11½ years old, 1982.

GRANDMOTHER'S STORIES

JOHN'S STORY

Gary and Becky Armstrong were John's dearest playmates. They lived across the alley from us in an apartment in their grandmother's home. Gary and John were of the same age. Becky was a year younger. They were quiet, well-behaved children. They came to our house often and particularly on Saturday nights when I read Bible stories to JoAnn and John. Many evenings just at sundown we would hear a soft knock on the door. Gary and Becky would be standing there hand in hand. Gary would always say, "Can we come in and hear the Bible stories?"

I let them in for sundown worship. We began by singing, "This Little Light of Mine" and "Zaccheus Was a Wee Little Man." These were great favorites with Gary and Becky. We followed our singing with a Bible story and pictures. Then we all knelt for prayer. Worship over, Gary would take Becky by the hand and they would leave as softly and quietly as they came. I always marveled at these little visits. I felt God's guidance and the working of the Holy Spirit in our neighborhood.

One hot summer day John and Gary were playing in the alley. The bees were busy building a nest on the corner of our garage. With big sticks in hand, John and Gary were hitting at the bees. Gary swung the stick. John looked up to see which bee was going down next. The stick missed the bee and hit John in the open eye. I heard John screaming and I ran out into the alley. Gary's mother came running out, too. She backed her car out of the garage. I held a wet wash cloth over John's eye and we went speeding to the doctor. Dr. Kieth, our family doctor, made an appointment for us to see an eye specialist. We arrived there shortly. He put John on the examining table. He turned on the overhead light. He said it would be necessary to take stitches in the eye and he would not be able to give an anesthetic. He said that John would have to look up and hold his eye in a steady position while he took the stitches.

I knew this was a time for more prayer. The doctor left the room to prepare for the operation. John and I had time to make our requests known to God. We prayed together. John was calm and ready when the doctor came in with his needle and thread. He held his eye open and steady while the stitches were quickly taken. The doctor praised John for his bravery and courage and rewarded him with an all-day sucker.

The Holy Spirit is our guide and our comforter. God is our strength and ever-present help in time of trouble.

John graduated from Oak Park Academy in May of 1969. John stayed home for the summer and worked on a construction job, saving his money for college. He chose Union College in Lincoln, Nebraska. In the fall he began a four-year course in business.

Joy Wallman, John's special friend from academy days, was also college-bound. Joy, too, headed for Union College where she began a four-year course in nursing.

John and Joy continued dating. At the end of their junior year they began talking of marriage. In July of 1972 the family gathered at Lincoln, Nebraska, for the wedding. Elder Felton, principal of Oak Park Academy, performed the marriage ceremony. Joy wore an empire ivory gown of delustered satin and pleated chiffon. Jeweled lace accented the sleeves, skirt and train. She wore an elbow-length veil attached to a Juliet headpiece. Joy carried a bouquet of gardenias. Joy was now a Clemenson. We were all happy to welcome her, our newest addition to our family, and to love and cherish her forever.

Joy had a year of nursing to complete. She finished her training at the Porter Hospital in Denver, Colorado. John and Joy began their married life in Denver. John worked at construction. Joy earned her degree in nursing. John studied, and on a part-time schedule, he completed his business course.

Two sons joined them during these busy years. Christopher John was born on March 19, 1978. Shaun Matthew was born on January 5, 1980.

I enjoyed many weeks of my summer vacation with Chris and Shaun in Denver. We went on picnics. We went hiking and swimming. But the most fun of all was the way we liked to catch frogs. Every morning after breakfast we would take some water in a pail and go to the drainage ditch frog hunting. The frogs usually hid in the grass beside the ditch. We would have to sit down and be very still and watch for one to hop up. Then, quick as a flash, we would grab one. One has to be very quick to be quicker than a frog. Shaun liked to put his frogs in the wading pool, then jump in with them. After a nice swim together he dumped them all out in the grass and they disappeared in the ditch. The next morning we went out with our pails to catch them all over again.

There were snakes in the ditch, too. Chris learned to catch them by the tail. His first catch was quite exciting. He hung onto it tight and ran to the kitchen to show his mother. Mother didn't share his enthusiasm for snakes. "You get that snake out of this house at once!" she yelled. Chris wanted to keep it. He put it in a cardboard box with some crumpled newspapers. The snake got out and hid behind some boxes in the garage. Later we saw him crawling under the porch. Chris decided to let the snake have his freedom.

Another one of our favorite things to do was to sit in the yard and watch the

GRANDMOTHER'S STORIES

lightning. Storms had a way of blowing in suddenly over the foothills. Streak lightning flashed across the sky over the mountains. Lightning was followed by a crash of thunder. The wind began to blow a gale whipping the branches of the trees and blowing the birds out of the sky. The rain finally came down in torrents, chasing us into the house. Shaun loved to watch these storms and when he saw a bit of lightning in the sky he would say, "Come, Grandma, let's watch the funder."

Chris and Shaun grew bigger and taller every summer. They are busy these days working on their honor badges, camping and swimming with the Pathfinders.

John has part ownership in a construction company, Cement Foundations, in Littleton, Colorado.

Christophor and Shaun Clemenson, catching frogs, Littleton, Colorado.

Elise, Ben and Shoshonnah Dickerson and their pet goat on their farm at Garrison, Iowa.

GRACE CLEMENSON

John and Joy Clemenson wedding, 1972.

Christopher Clemenson, 3½ years. Shaun Clemenson, 8 months.

GRANDMOTHER'S STORIES

MAVIS' STORY

Mavis Jacobson came to our home to live when she was about eight years old. Dora, Gerhart's sister, was Mavis's mother. Dora lived near us in Marion. Mavis was a pretty little red-haired girl with big blue eyes and a friendly smile. She lived with her father in Chicago. Her father was divorced from his second wife and he and Mavis were living in a boarding home run by an adventist friend, Aunt Marion. Aunt Marion became Mavis's baby-sitter and second mother.

Mavis began to coax her dad to bring her to Marion. She knew her real mother was living there, and she was becoming curious. One day they came. Mother and daughter gazed at one another in wonder. They had the same red hair, blue eyes, and wide open smile. We fell in love with Mavis at once. Her father wanted us to keep her for the summer. Summer turned to fall and her father came back to take her on a trip to Minnesota. He then took her back to Chicago to live.

Mavis was unhappy now. She had enjoyed her stay with us and wanted to come back. She came quite unexpectedly one day in January. Aunt Marion brought her bag and baggage. She stated that for various reasons Mavis could no longer live with her dad. We would have to keep her. We were overjoyed! We made sure that she never left us again. She stayed until she was married at the age of nineteen.

We now had three little young people to care for. John was seven years old, Mavis was eight, and JoAnn was nine. After an adjustment period of a few fights and some struggles among the children, we settled down to peaceful living. The children were all assigned daily chores. We had a bathroom which needed cleaning, rugs to vaccum, dishes to wash, beds to make, garbage to carry out, trash to burn, and clothes to hang out on wash day. All of this was children's work. There was play time, too. In the winter there was sledding on a near-by hill. In summer they took swimming lessons. On Mondays, Wednesdays, and Fridays after the morning work was done, JoAnn, Mavis, and John grabbed a sack lunch and their swimming suits and raced for the pool. After lessons were over, they stayed and played for the afternoon. JoAnn and Mavis took piano lessons. They bought patterns and material and sewed their school clothes on my old pedal sewing machine. They liked to bake and decorate fancy cakes. They helped in the garden and helped with the canning. They did baby-sitting, too, and saved their money for a trip to Chicago to visit Aunt Marion. They sewed matching dresses for this occasion. They had a grand vacation riding the train and sight-seeing in Chicago.

We were a hard-working family. We all kept busy with our own projects. One summer Gary and Vern planted a five-cent package of pumpkin seeds. It was a good year for pumpkins. At picking time we had a great pile of pumpkins in our back yard. Kids going to and from school bought their jack-o-lanterns. One day our grocery man came to deliver groceries. He bought the remainder of the pile at twenty-five cents apiece. Gary and Vern cleared fifty dollars on their pumpkin patch that year.

The children all earned and saved money for summer camp. There was money to be made in the little city of Marion, and the Clemenson clan could think of ways to earn it. We raised corn in our garden. Mavis, JoAnn, and John piled it in their wagon and pulled it around the neighborhood selling it for fifty cents a dozen.

The winter snows created work of shoveling. After a big two-day snow storm, many times school would be closed. Mavis, JoAnn, and John jumped out of bed early. After a hurried breakfast they took up their shovels and started out. All day they went door to door, shoveling snow as they went. At the end of the day they came home excitedly counting their money and dropped it into their banks.

Mavis graduated from Oak Park Academy in May of 1968. She came home and found work for the summer..

Mavis had been dating Ed Dickerson during their academy days. Now that they were graduated they wanted to get married. In December of 1968 we planned a Christmas wedding. Mavis bought yards and yards of white velveteen. How well I remember the evenings we spent sitting on Mavis' bed sewing on the jeweled braid which trimmed the neck line, sleeves and train. She wore an elbow-length veil which was attached to a crown accented with Jeweled braid. Mavis carried a bouquet of red roses and white carnations. Gerhart gave the bride away. JoAnn was matron of honor. Mavis sang the *Song of Ruth* which brought tears to our eyes and the wedding to a beautiful and impressive close.

In the fall of 1969, Mavis and Ed moved to Bemidji, Minnesota, where Ed began his teaching career. Ed attended summer school each summer, and in 1981 he graduated from Andrews University with a Masters in Education.

During these years Mavis became a home-maker and mother. Ben was born on March 19, 1978. Shoshannah was born on July 4, 1980. Elise was born on October 29, 1984. They enjoy the freedom of country living with goats, chickens, ducks, dogs and cats.

In the summer of 1986, Chris and I flew to Iowa to spend a week with them on the farm. We played ball, built fences, and herded goats. We roasted marshmallows over a bonfire. Chris and I agreed that we had a grand and happy time that week on the farm with Ben, Shoshonnah and Elise.

Mavis is a home-make, wife and mother to her three children and husband Ed in Garrison, Iowa.

GRANDMOTHER'S STORIES

Mavis and Ed Dickerson wedding, 1968.

Mavis Jacobson, the bride and JoAnn Newhard, the bridesmaid, Mavis' wedding, 1968.

Elise, Benjamin and Shoshannah Dickerson.

GRACE CLEMENSON

Patty Jo Clemenson and John Brown.

Grace Clemenson and Eileen Murphy at JoAnn's wedding, 1968.

Betty Clemenson, Grace Clemenson in back ground at JoAnn's wedding, 1968.

GRANDMOTHER'S STORIES

GERHART'S RETIREMENT YEARS

In the spring of 1967, Gerhart had a massive heart attack. He survived, but was never able to work again. He retired from the police force in the summer of that year.

Gerhart was happy in his retirement years, and developed several hobbies. The first and most important hobby was antique hunting with his friend, John Brunen. They went to farm sales where Gerhart bought antique tools and machinery, old chairs, kitchen gadgets and crockery. The greatest find of all, and one I treasure to this day, is an antique trunk. I refinished it inside and out, and keep it with me at all times. I store my homemade quilts in it, and enjoy the fresh cedar fragrance.

Gerhart became interested in mushroom hunting with his friend, Bill Brunen. Bill grew up in the Central City area. He knew all the mushrooms and their secret hiding places. Gerhart learned to identify seven kinds of mushrooms. He brought them home, cleaned them, sauteed them, boiled them, fried them, froze them and pickled them. It was a fun and rewarding hobby.

I didn't always trust the looks of some of the mushrooms, and doubted that we should be eating them. One evening Gerhart sauteed a panful of something white he called cottage cheese. He said it grew on the side of trees. He filled his plate and began to eat. I watched him for a minute, then I said, "Well, if your are going, I am going, too." I ate my helping. The next morning I awoke to find us both alive and well.

Gerhart included traveling as a part of his retirement. We took two train trips to the West Coast, visiting relatives. Gerhart and Vern took a trip together in the summer of 1967. They, too, went west to Seattle. Gerhart stayed most of the summer with Aunt Laura.

One September day the telephone rang. It was Crystal. "We are coming for a visit," she informed me. "We will be there tomorrow afternoon." They came in their Ford Mercury station wagon. When they arrived, Chuck said, "Grace, I want to see how well you can drive." I had been taking driving lessons and was having a bad time with our old stick shift. Chuck gave me his keys and said, "You can do the driving."

I drove out into the country and around town. When we arrived home, Chuck said, "Now you can keep the keys. The car is yours." I was astounded. Now we had a car with power steering, power windows, and air conditioning. This car was only four years old, and a dream to drive. Crystal and Chuck flew back to Minneapolis the next day. Gerhart and I began planning a trip to Spokane to see Vern, Judy, and Scott.

We took many grand and happy trips in our Ford Mercury station wagon. We traveled to Great Falls to visit Maurice and Wanda whom we had not seen for thirty years. We went to Conrad, Montana, to see Gerhart's Uncle Carl and Aunt Clara. On one of our winter trips across Wyoming, we were snowed in for two days with our friends, Perry and Sherma Wells. We took frequent short trips to Minnesota and North Dakota. On many of these trips we took our camping gear, our bedrolls, cooking utensils, and our Coleman stove. KOA campgrounds were our favorite stopping places. We unloaded our groceries, dishes, and stove on a table. We made up our beds in the back of the station wagon. After supper and clean-up we went to bed to watch the stars come out. We listened to the night sounds of birds settling down, and crickets that kept up their chirping all through the night.

We liked to rise with the sun. It is the most beautiful time of day to travel. Quietly we dressed, packed and loaded. Quietly we left. This is a quiet time of day; few cars are out. Many little wild creatures are seeking an early morning breakfast. How well I remember the thrill of seeing a flock of wild turkeys by the roadside. Antelope and deer were a common sight grazing on the prairie grasses. One time we stopped to watch a band of coyotes making a sneak attack on a herd of antelope. They were anticipating a big breakfast of antelope meat. They were disappointed. On hearing the faint rustle of the grass, the leader of the herd raised his head, gave a signal of alarm, and they were off. The coyotes made a short chase and gave up. We watched as the antelope leaped to safety and the coyotes made their return trip through the tall grass and over the hill.

Now Gerhart and I were hungry for our breakfast. We began watching for the early morning opening of a roadside cafe. Soon we were eating our breakfast of hash-brown potatoes and fried eggs, toast, juice, milk, and coffee. After breakfast we were off again enjoying the scenery and freedom from care and worry. When our five children were growing up, we stayed home while they were out chasing. JoAnn once said to me, "Mother, there was a time when you and Dad never knew where we were. Now it's our turn to worry about you, for we never know where you are."

Gerhart was always proud to be a member of the Marion Police force. Upon his retirement in 1967 he received this letter of appreciation from the American Legion for work well done.

Our trip west in our Ford Mercury station wagon, July 1969.

GRANDMOTHER'S STORIES

American Legion Post #258 page2 May 2, 1967

Officer Clemenson has always taken pride in being a member of the Police Department and a part of the fast growing city. His record will show that, over the years, he has never had an accident with city vehicles, there has never been a vehicle or piece of equipment damaged due to his negligence and the most outstanding of all, is that there has never been a valid complaint against Officer Clemenson in spite of all the controversial situations that he has had to cope with. The only complaint against Officer Clemenson was that lodged by a drunk driver who complained the next day that Officer Clemenson had taken him from a bar stool in a tavern and had charged him with drunk driving. The facts were that the complaintant was considerably more intoxicated than he realized and was in fact driving when arrested.

Officer Clemenson, along with his other duties, has for the past several years taken the chairmanship of the Annual Dance committee and has each year carried this to a rousing success.

Officer Clemenson is well liked by his fellow officers and it is not unusual to hear a comment made to the effect that the presence of Officer Clemenson, in a particular situation, was quite comforting.

Over the years, Officer Clemenson has demonstrated his consistent reliability, his ability to cope with adverse situations, his ability to deal with people under conditions of stress and still come up with a solution generally agreeable to all and at the same time retain the respect of those with whom he has had to deal. His faithfulness to the Department, his loyalty to his fellow officers, his devotion to duty are certainly some of the outstanding qualities of this fine officer and if I may, as Chief of Police, say that I am most happy to be able to recommend him as the OUTSTANDING OFFICER OF THIS DEPARTMENT.

Officer Clemenson recently suffered a heart attack and is presently confined at St. Lukes Hospital in Cedar Rapids.

Officer Clemenson and his wife Grace have four children, Gary, Vern, Joan and John. They are at home at 960 18th Street, Marion.

Sincerely,
Leighton W. Ford
Chief of Police

GRACE CLEMENSON

PRESENTED TO
"CLEM"

GEARHART 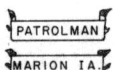 CLEMENSON

FOR OUTSTANDING SERVICE TO HIS COMMUNITY THROUGH CARRYING OUT HIS DUTIES AS A POLICE OFFICER IN A MANNER WHICH REFLECTS CREDIT UPON ALL POLICE OFFICERS AND FOR DEDICATION TO HIS PROFESSION ABOVE AND BEYOND THE CALL OF DUTY.

E. A. BLACKMORE
NATIONAL ADJUTANT

JOHN E. DAVIS
NATIONAL COMMANDER

POST ADJUTANT

POST COMMANDER

Marion POST NO. 298 DEPARTMENT OF Iowa

NATIONAL HEADQUARTERS OF THE AMERICAN LEGION, INDIANAPOLIS, INDIANA, June 7, 1967

Police Chief Leighton Ford, Officer Gerhart Clemenson, Mayor Potter and James Klaner. Mayor Potter presenting award of achievement to Officer Clemenson for outstanding service to his community. June 7, 1967.

GRANDMOTHER'S STORIES

GRANDMOTHER'S HOBBIES

During these retirement years I was busy with my own hobbies. When JoAnn and Mavis left home, the piano sat quietly in one corner of the family room. I missed the sound of the practice. The house seemed so quiet. I decided that I would learn to play the piano. I got the book *Michael Arrons Adult Beginners*. I played it through several times. Soon I was able to play my first hymn, "Sitting at the Feet of Jesus," and my second hymn, "What a Friend We Have in Jesus." From there I went on and on learning new hymns.

I had always had an interest in poetry. How well I remember myself as a teen-ager, taking trips to the library and checking out books of poetry. At home in my room I read them through and through. I read poetry out loud, too, to my sister and my friends and anyone who would listen. Now I began to write poetry of my own. One fall as I stood looking out of my kitchen window I saw black clouds rolling in from the north. The wind was blowing a gale, and the birds were sailing sideways, flowing along with the current. Trash, bits of paper, and leaves were whirling and twirling in the alley. I picked up my pen and wrote my first verse.

THIS IS FALL

Honking gray geese, flying high,
Snowflakes swirling in the sky,
Black clouds rolling from the north,
Bringing threats of gale and wintry wrath.
Puddles icy, trees are bare,
Blackbirds scattering everywhere.
Dry leaves make a rustling sound,
Winter showing all around.
God's changing hand is over all,
Summer is gone; this is fall.

I wrote another one on fall at a later date which I like better. This one is entitled God Gave Us Fall.

GRACE CLEMENSON

GOD GAVE US FALL

God gave us fall that we might see
The plan of His creativity,
First the bud and then the bloom
Then in the fall like an ancient tomb
They crumble and fall into the dust
And become a part of the universe.

We watch the geese in wonderment,
As they sail across the firmament.
We cannot see God's presence there,
But know He guides them through the air,
How could they know which way to go
If God did not arrange them so.

If we would follow where God leads
He would supply our every need.
The bees and birds and flowers and us
He keeps us all within his trust.
God gave us fall to understand
We too, are lead by a mighty Hand.

That winter the cold winds blew outside the door. The cold chill of winter crept into the corners of the kitchen. I felt impressed to write again.

WINTER COMPARISONS

Winter is an angry wolf
Hanging around the door
Howling, puffing to get in
And chill us to the core.
He tramps the icy road at night,
We hear him howling round.
As we are wrapped up warm in bed
He runs the frozen ground.

Winter is a wretched witch
With fingers long and grasping,
She tears your hair and chills your bones

GRANDMOTHER'S STORIES

Her screams are loud and rasping.
She haunts you in the night-time
She rattles at your shutters,
She rustles up and down the lawn
She grumbles and she mutters.

Winter is an artist
Painting window panes,
Drawing ancient castles
And leaves with lacy veins.
With his brush and palette
He works with icy hand,
Then dries it with his frosty breath
Bright pictures for the land.

My poem on spring was written as I watched the jonquils pushing their heads out from their winter beds as the sun and rain beat down on them, and the March winds cruelly battered them from side to side. My poem "Salute to Spring" was born so naturally, so easily.

SALUTE TO SPRING

Spring, I salute you as you come in,
Your banners fluttering in the March wind.
You pick up the paper and pieces of trash,
Carry them high, then drip with a crash.
Then you twirl them round and round and round
Then hold them still upon the ground.
Good-bye to the lion, Hello to the lamb
Spring, you are master of all you command.

Spring I salute you as you slip in,
Soft and silent on an April rain.
Suddenly the sun comes creeping out
From behind a black cloud, and looks about.
The violets lift up their heads
Jack-in-the-pulpit leaps from his bed.
The first blade of grass, the robin sings
Pease and contentment to all it brings.
Then a volley of thunder, like a mighty drum
And a thought like a flash of lightning comes
God's your Commander, and He's watching you
God's my Commander, and He sees me through.

GRACE CLEMENSON

GRANDMOTHER'S SKETCHES

For several years my interest turned to sketching. I carried a pad and pencil with me at all times. I liked to sketch log cabins, churches and barns. These were my favorites. You will find them here in this book.

One day Gerhart and I were driving past the Little Brown Church in Nashua, Iowa. We stopped to admire the old fashioned structure. I took out my pad and pencil and standing by the side of the road, made a quick sketch. Several years later I took the sketch to an art class and made a finished product of my own view of the Little Brown Church.

The same was done with my mother's log cabin on the front cover and the Iowa barns.

The Little Brown Church, Nashua, Iowa, Chicksaw County, by Grace Clemenson.

GRANDMOTHER'S STORIES

Iowa Barn, Story County, Iowa.

GRACE CLEMENSON

An old pump still stands one mile south of Shellsburg in Benton County, Iowa.

GRANDMOTHER'S STORIES

Iowa Barn, Story County, Iowa.

GRACE CLEMENSON

GRANDMOTHER'S RECIPES

Collecting and trying new recipes has been a hobby of mine for many years. Some I try and discard. Some I keep. They became favorites with family and friends. The five I have included in my book are very special, with you, my grandchildren. Someday you can open this book and begin stirring up a batch of Sugar and Spice Cinnamon Rolls or put together a Rhubarb Crunch.

SUGAR and SPICE CINNAMON ROLLS

1 package yeast
½ cup warm water
½ cup butter
⅓ cup sugar
4-4½ cups flour

1 teaspoon salt
1 cup hot scalded milk
1 unbeaten egg, room temperature
½ cup Malt-O-Meal

Dissolve yeast in water. Combine butter, sugar, salt and scalded milk. Cool to luke-warm. Blend in egg and yeast. Beat until smooth. Add remaining flour to make a stiff dough. Cover, let rise in a warm place about 1½ hours. Divide dough into two balls. Roll each into a 7½ inch rectangle on lightly floured board. Brush with melted butter. Sprinkle with cinnamon sugar. Roll and cut. Place cut pieces into greased muffin tins, let rise. Bake 35-40 minutes in 300° oven.

CREAMY MACARONI and CHEESE BAKE

2 cups uncooked macaroni
⅓ cup mayonnaise
¼ cup chopped pimento
¼ cup chopped green pepper
¼ cup finely chopped onion
1 can condensed Cream of Mushroom soup
½ cup milk
1 cup shredded Velveeta Spread

Cook macaroni according to package directions; drain. Combine with next four ingredients. Blend soup, milk, and cheese. Stir into macaroni. Pour into one quart casserole.

Bake uncovered at 300° for 25 minutes. Makes 4 - 6 servings.

GRANDMOTHER'S STORIES

OATMEAL PIE

3 well beaten eggs
⅔ cup sugar
1 cup brown sugar
⅔ cup quick oats (uncooked)
⅔ cup coconut and ⅔ cup chopped walnuts
2 Tbs. butter, melted
1 tsp. Vanilla

Mix ingredients together and pour into unbaked pie shell.
Bake 30 minutes at 350°

OATMEAL BURGER HOT DISH

2 eggs beaten
1 cup toasted bread crumbs
1 cup uncooked oatmeal
1 cup cottage cheese
1 onion grated
2 tablespoons margarine, melted
½ tsp. poultry seasoning

Combine all ingredients, form into patties, brown lightly. Place in casserole and cover with mushroom or celery soup and simmer in oven.

RHUBARB CRUNCH

1 cup sifted flour
¾ cup oatmean (uncooked)
1 cup brown sugar
½ cup melted butter
1 tsp. cinnamon

Mix above ingredients until crumbly. Press half of crumbs in greased baking pan, cover with 4 cups diced rhubarb.

1 cup sugar   2 Tbs. cornstarch
1 cup water   1 tsp. vanilla

Combine these and cook until thick and clear. Pour over rhubarb. Top with a few of the crumbs. Bake in moderate oven 300° for one hour. Cut into squares and serve warm, plain, or with whipped cream.

GRACE CLEMENSON

GERHART'S CONVERSION

During his busy working years, Gerhart had not taken any interest in his salvation. Now that he was retired, I felt that he should take time to open the Bible and read and pray with me. I asked him several times. His answer was always a firm, "No."

When he was in the hospital for a six-weeks stay with a heart attack, I wanted so much to bring God's Word to him. There was no time or place for reading God's Word there. His room was a busy, noisy place. Too many visitors were coming and going. Gerhart was popular in our small town. Friends and well-wishers literally flooded his room. There were times when I asked to have a NO VISITORS sign put up to give him some rest. I called the Police Chief, Leighton Ford, and the fire chief, Jim Reynolds, and asked them to instruct their men to control their visits. I never had a private moment with Gerhart as long as he was in the hospital. When I walked in, there was always someone there. When I kissed him good-night, there was someone watching. Gerhart attracted people like a magnet. The teenagers in town loved him because of his interest in them, his corrections, and his counseling and love for them. They called him "Dad" and their love and affection overflowed in cards and visits.

I was thinking only of his salvation. I began writing out Bible verses on slips of paper and folding them into little bits. I would leave them in his hand when I said good-night. He told me later that he read them all. After a six-weeks stay in the hospital, Gerhart came home. He made contact with friends and began to establish a life of retirement.

One Sunday night, as John and Mavis were preparing to return to the academy, I made a special Sunday night supper for them. Gary, Sharon, Kimberly, JoAnn, J.R., and Michelle were all with us. Gerhart was visiting friends in Central City. His place at the table was empty.

I felt that this was the time to discuss with the children a question I had on my mind. I had a constant feeling that Gerhart might drop dead at any time. I wondered how we should plan the funeral. I wanted them to give me their suggestions. We decided to have Mr. Baxter handle the funeral service. The Marion Policemen were to be pallbearers. We decided to ask Shirley Brettheour to be the organist. We made a list of people to notify. I wrote this all down and tucked it into the pocket of a calendar. Tears came to my eyes as I cautioned the children that they must never tell their dad what we had done. I felt that he would be upset and angry.

During that coming week I felt a heavy burden to pray for Gerhart. I told the Lord that I had done all that I could think of to do for him. I said, "He is in Your hands now, Lord. Please show me anything else I can do to help him. I will do anything you tell me to do." I prayed this prayer on Wednesday, Thursday and Friday nights. On Sabbath I went to church. We knelt for prayer. I asked the Lord again to show me what more I could do for my dear husband. As I was kneeling there and praying, these words went before my eyes. "Tell him the plans you made for his funeral." This was the very thing I thought I should not do. But the Lord had spoken. "Yes, dear Lord, I will tell him."

As JoAnn and I drove home from church that day I felt I was sailing on a cloud. God had shown me what to do. I felt that Gerhart was already among the saved. At home I prepared our lunch. As we were eating, Gerhart asked me if I would like to ride out into the country to visit our friends, the Stienhooks. We drove out the River Road, a beautiful scenic drive. The message I had to give Gerhart was shelved in the back of my mind. I did not know how I was going to approach Gerhart on this subject. I needed an opening. I did not know how it would come about. God knew, and He soon showed me. We arrived at the Stienhook farmhouse. As we walked into the kitchen, we found the family seated around the kitchen table making plans for a funeral. Gerret's brother had died during the night. We sat with them and talked about funeral homes, pastors and cemeteries. Gerhart and I finally left and walked out to the car. I knew now that I had the opening I had been waiting for. Before Gerhart started the car, I said to him, "Gerhart, there is something I want to talk over with you. When the children were home last weekend we made plans for your funeral." He said, "Good, tell me about it." I related the plans to him. We had not decided on a pastor. Gerhart was a Lutheran and I asked him if he wanted a Lutheran pastor. He said, "No, I want Reverend Moore to preach my funeral sermon. He is a Baptist minister and a good friend of mine." I asked him if Pastor Moore ever talked to him about his salvation. "No," Gerhart said. "We just talk and joke."

"Well, I want to tell you something," I answered. "We are not saved by pastors, we are not saved by churches, we are not saved by families. We are saved only through our personal relationship with Jesus. This is something that you and I need to be working on. Would you be willing to go home now and open the Bible and pray with me?" Gerhart said, "Yes, I would."

From that day on Gerhart and I had worship together every day. Soon I noticed changes taking place, denoting the working of the Holy Spirit. He became more relaxed. His angers and frustrations disappeared. He spent much time listening to

GRACE CLEMENSON

Christian music. He began a prayer life of his own.

Gerhart was raised in the Norwegian Luterhan faith. He spent three years as a young boy studying the Lutheran Catechism. He knew the Bible well. The Holy Spirit was working strongly in his life. When he died on March 5, 1974, we had a funeral at Baxter's Funeral Home in Marion. Gary made the funeral arrangements, carrying out the plans we had agreed upon. From Marion we took him to his home town for burial. He is lying in the little churchyard cemetery of the Norwegian Lutheran Church in Gonvick, Minnesota where he was confirmed. He is resting on a lot with his father and mother. My place is there, too, and someday I will join them. We will sleep there until Jesus comes. The Bible says, "Train up a child in the way he should go, and when he is old he will not depart from it." Proverbs 22:6. God's promises never fail.

Gerhart C. Clemenson, 960 18th Street, Marion, Iowa, 1967.

Cemetery, 1974. Gonvick, Minnesota, Gerhart's resting place.

The Clemenson Stone, Gonvick Cemetery, Gonvick, Minnesota.

GRANDMOTHER'S STORIES

OUR MOVE TO SPOKANE

The fall of 1972 came. Gerhart and I had been married for thirty-four years. For twenty-four of those years we had lived in Marion, our favorite corner of the earth.

Many changes had taken place in the old home at 960 18th street. The walls once vibrated with the cries and coos of a baby. John was born there. JoAnn, as a toddler, once explored the rooms and halls. Gary and Vern, our school-age boys, held pillow fights in their bedroom and built snow forts in the back yard. Our cocker spaniel, Susie, rushed to keep up.

The children became teen-agers, as all children do. The old home resounded with teen-age liveliness. We had raised five of them and had experienced our share of struggles - struggles with dating, driving, partying, and school activities. In no time at all the wedding bells began to ring. One by one our children, now grown, marched down the aisle and out into the world.

Gerhart and I began to build a new life together. Gerhart continued on with his hobbies. Antique collecting and mushroom hunting were two of them. Berry picking and camping filled our summer days. In the winter we visited friends and went ice fishing. How well I remember fishing through a hole in the ice on the Cedar River. Fishing contests were held at Central City during the month of January. They continued on for several weekends. A prize was given for the largest fish caught. Lunch was served in tents pitched along the banks of the river.

Our preparation for these trips was quite extensive. We were up and out of bed early on Sunday morning. We ate heartily of a breakfast of scrambled eggs with mushrooms, toast and coffee. Gerhart loaded the car with our fishing gear, extra socks, mittens, long johns, camp-stools, kindling wood, and matches.

We found our friends, Margret and Ob, searching the ice for a good fishing spot. We picked our spot and settled down next to them. With a special tool, Gerhart and Ob cut holes in the ice. Margret and I carried wood and built the fires. I hung up a kettle for hot water. We sat down on our camp stools and dropped our lines into the hole. There we sat waiting patiently for a bite. We did not wait long. Suddenly Gerhart felt a tug on his line. He pulled up a two-pound catfish, then dropped it back into the hole. The fire needed more wood. The water was hot. Margret and Ob joined us for a cup of hot tea. Soon it was noon. We all went to the tent for lunch. Two hours were taken up at the lunch counter, eating and visiting.

GRACE CLEMENSON

The sun set early in winter. At four o'clock we packed up and went home. We caught no fish but our lungs caught plenty of cold, fresh air. We had the joy of a good social time in the out-of-doors. Next Sunday we would go again.

Summers in Iowa were hot and humid. Gerhart began to talk of moving to a cooler climate. Vern and Judy lived in Spokane. We had visited there several times. Gerhart was suffering continually from heart problems since his first heart attack. The high altitude, the lighter air, and mild climate of Spokane appealed to him. He experienced relief with his breathing problem and felt comfortable in the drier climate. Gerhart was sure that a move to Spokane would be right for him. I was not so sure. I felt some misgivings at leaving family and friends so far behind. I asked him how he felt about it. His answer was, "We can always make new friends." These words were to come back to me many times in those lonely months after Gerhart's death.

We arrived in Spokane on February 12, 1974. Gerhart died on March 5 of that same year. I still marvel at God's goodness in settling me down in a neighborhood of friendly, caring people. The Kellys, Annie and Ralph, lived across the street from me. The first time I talked to Annie she said to me, "Do you have a church home? We would be happy to have you worship with us." They are a praying family and were a consistant help and comfort to me. Ann and Jack Chadwell were near and dear neighbors. They became close friends. I see them often. Emogene and Mick Jacobson lived next door. They visited me often. They helped me make decisions, taught me the tricks of Western gardening, and helped me find my way around the strange new city.

I began attending church at the Spokane Valley Seventh Day Advent Church. Lurlie Bagwell was one of the first to greet me. She invited me to attend her afternoon prayer group. She soon became one of my near and dear friends.

Carol Bagwell taught school at the Valley church school. I became well acquainted with her as we took three art classes together. I spent many happy hours with Lurlie and Carol in their home. They patiently listened to *"Grandmother's Stories,"* as they unfolded. We laughed and cried together as we revised sentences and corrected spellings. I am deeply grateful to them for their friendship and help.

In September I began job hunting in Spokane. In no time at all I found work as a cook's helper at the University Manor Convalescent Home. I began some new and interesting work, learning to cook institutional food, learning to read diet cards, and to cook and serve food for diabetics, purees, and salt frees. I discovered some interesting and intelligent people living out their last days within the confines of the home. They were people with faith, courage, and a sense of humor. One little lady came into the kitchen every morning to greet the kitchen crew and to snitch a cookie which I thoughtfully left on the counter. She would talk a while, pick up the cookies, and shuffle back to her room to eat them.

I organized a Bible study group with twelve to fifteen meeting in the dining room. They brought their Bibles, looked up texts, sang hymns, and said a prayer. When one of the group became ill with a liver ailment and was confined to her room, I was able to minister to her. She had no church home, no pastor, and no family. I visited her every day for several weeks before her death. I knew her favorite hymn, her favorite scriptures, and how she loved the Lord. I was there when she breathed her last breath. Her pain and suffering was over. She will sleep in peace until Jesus comes to call her home. I know I shall see her again someday in the beautiful earth made new.

Kimberly Clemenson and Brenda Clemenson taken on our acreage in Iowa about 1972.

Expo 1974; Judy, Scott, Gary, John, Sharon, Kim and Brenda Clemenson.

Expo 1974; Vern and Scott Clemenson.

Expo 1974; Scott Clemenson, Michelle and JoAnn Newhard.

GRANDMOTHER'S STORIES

EXPO '74

In the summer of 1974, Spokane hosted the World's Fair. For six months the eyes of the world gazed upon Spokane, a city of one hundred and eighty thousand, the smallest city ever to host a world exposition.

I bought a season ticket and spent many hours brousing through the displays. I especially enjoyed the Korean Dancers and their traditional folk dance program. Steeped in folk lore, they danced the Flower Dance, the Monk Dance, the Fan Dance, and many others. The U.S. Pavilion and the Imax Theater, the Washington State Pavilion, and the Smithsonian Folk Exhibits were high on my list of priorities. The USSR had a mammoth display which I visited several times. The Republic of China was a great favorite of mine. Through a film I learned how the people of modern day Taiwan eat, dress, work, and play.

The highlight of the summer occurred when I took my friends, Irene and Harold Bliss and their daughter Coreen, on a one-day guided tour. With Kim accompanying us, we walked all day exploring and enjoying the sights. We found a fruit stand where we stopped to lunch on melon and strawberries. We sat on a park bench and listened to the Heritage Singers singing our favorite hymns.

We arrived home at eleven o'clock. Kim and Coreen went straight to bed. Harold, Irene, and I sat around the kitchen table talking. Suddenly we heard a disturbance in the back yard. The neighbor's cows were in my garden. We ran out, drove the cows back into their own pasture, and with a flashlight we patched up the hole in the fence.

The next morning after worship and breakfast, Harold said that they must start for home. They loaded the car and said good-bye. Harold reached into his pocket for his glasses. They were gone. We all began to hunt. Irene searched the bedroom. Kim and Coreen looked through the living room and kitchen. Harold searched through the luggage. We walked through the garden and around the mended fence. We examined thoroughly each blade of grass and every stick and stone. The glasses were nowhere. Harold said that he could not drive home without them. He suggested that we should have prayer. We all knelt down in the field near the garden. Each one prayed that God in His Divine wisdom would give us the guidance we needed. We stood up and upon looking around I saw my little dog Bambi running toward me. I could see she was carrying something in her mouth. She ran up to me and dropped Harold's glasses at my feet. We knelt down again and thanked God for His help. When we have exhausted all of our knowledge and abilities and completely lean on Him, He will not let us down. Our extremity is God's opportunity. Harold put his glasses on. They said good-bye again and started back to their home in Iowa. I continued on with my guided tours until I had visited EXPO more than twenty times. JoAnn, Ron and Michelle came from Zearing, Iowa. Gary, Sharon, Kim amd Brenda visited me that summer from Cedar Rapids, Iowa. Crystal and Chuck flew in from Minneapolis. John and Joy visited from Denver. All were anxious for a sight seeing trip through the EXPO grounds. I thoroughly enjoyed the summer and it was with mixed feelings that I watched the closing of the World's Exposition in October.

Brooke Asbury, age 5.

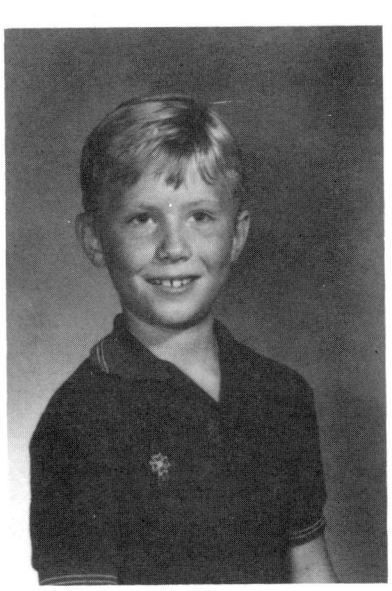

Ben Asbury, age 8.

GRANDMOTHER'S STORIES

BEN AND BROOKE ASBURY

I worked at the nursing home for six years. It was hard, fast work. I was becoming exhausted and decided to look for other work. I searched the paper for a babysitting job. I prayed that God would guide me to the right position. Barbra Asbury, a young working mother with two small children, was also praying for the right person for her children. One Sunday afternoon I went to the home for an interview. We both felt that God was guiding, and I began what proved to be six years of service to the family.

I first saw Ben one Sunday afternoon when I went to the home to talk to his mother about the care of the children. Ben was three years old. He watched me from the shelter of his daddy's lap. Ben had pretty blond hair, blue eyes and round, rosy cheeks. I smiled at him. He stared back with a serious expression of uncertainty.

Ben and I made friends fast. I discovered his greatest interest was his little library. We read stories by the hour. Jack in the Beanstalk killed the giant day after day. Frosty the Snowman danced and played with the children and finally melted away in the sunshine. Mother Goose rhymes and animal stories were great favorites.

Ben was three-and-a-half years old when I bought him his first workbook. He was excited over this, and called it his special project. He learned numbers and letters. We studied shapes, sizes and colors. We drew pictures together. We made cats, witches, and jack-o-lanterns to decorate the windows for Halloween. We made stars, bells, and snowflakes for Christmas decorations. In the fall we raked up piles of leaves and jumped in them. In the winter we played in the snow and made snowmen and snow forts.

How well I remember the scary experience we had when the truck caught on fire. One afternoon after lunch, Ben went outdoors to play. He climbed into the back of his daddy's truck and accidentally pulled on some wiring. Suddenly smoke came billowing out. Ben ran into the kitchen shouting "The truck's on fire!" I could see the smoke rolling past the back door. I quickly called the fire department. In minutes they were there and had the fire out. The damage resulted in some burned-out wiring and two scared people, Ben and me.

Brooke was three months old when I began to care for her. For several weeks she spent her time eating and sleeping. Later, as she grew a little older, I put her in her play pen. She spent all of her time trying to get out. When I let her out, she went straight to the cupboard and proceeded to empty it of all its plastic dishes. For several weeks I stepped and tripped over covers and bowls. They seemed more interesting to her than toys.

One of the things I remember best about Brooke was the way she liked to eat. She enjoyed her food, and it was a pleasure for both of us when lunch time came. Brooke would open her mouth after every bite like a little bird waiting for another worm. Like the mother bird, I would keep dropping the food in until finally it was all gone. I would say, "All gone, Brooke, all gone." Brooke wasn't happy about that. She would shake her head and kick her feet and hold her mouth open for another bite.

Brooke's little girl friend, Jill, came often to play, bringing her dainty little dolls and dolls clothes. They played for hours together, entertaining their dolls with tea parties and birthday parties. Each doll had a birthday once a year. Somehow the girls never forgot a birthday. I would be informed a day in advance that Lindsey would be one year old tomorrow. I bought little cup cakes and we put a candle in each one. We sang the Happy Birthday song. The dolls sat up stiff and tall and stared straight ahead as the little mothers blew out the candles for them and ate the cakes.

Brooke and I spent many happy hours at the library browsing through the books. Little Lion was a great favorite of Brooke's, and came home with us often. His daddy bought him a pair of red rubber boots to wear out in the rain. Little Lion had a scary adventure down by the river when he was chased by a crocodile. He had a cold one day and had to stay in bed. His mother gave him some bad tasting medicine. He fell asleep and was chased by a red rabbit who jumped on his bed and woke him up. Little Lion was a fascinating little creature. We read his adventure over and over.

Brooke had some bad colds, too, and she, too, did not like to take her medicine. I would camouflage it in a teaspoon of sugar. After half an aspirin and a long nap, Brooke would wake up and say, "Read me the story about *Little Lion and His Bad, Bad Cold.*"

We had many good times at the Walk-in-the-Wild Zoo. One day Grandma Asbury and Pepper went with us. We took our lunch and ate, sitting on some rocks near the river. It was the spring of the year, and the Spokane River was flowing full and fast. Suddenly Pepper ran down to the river's edge. He jumped up on a rock, lost his balance, and fell into the river. We all ran down to the river bank. We called to him, "Here, Pepper! Come, Pepper! Swim, Pepper" Pepper swam as hard as he could. Soon he came to a low, flat rock. He crawled up on it and jumped to dry land. Grandma Asbury had a towel ready to dry him off. He licked our hands as we hugged and petted him. Now that he was safe, we were all ready to go home, thankful and happy to have Pepper with us.

GRANDMOTHER'S STORIES

Tilly, my puppy, was not so fortunate. She was hit by a car and killed in front of the Asbury house. One evening Brooke and Ben and Tilly and I were playing on the front lawn. Mr. Ching, the little dog across the street, came out to play. Tilly ran across the street to touch noses with him. I called her to come home. She came running across the street just as a car came speeding around the corner. Tilly was hit and killed instantly. The car sped on. Ben, Brooke, and I ran out into the street to look at her. Tilly lay still and silent. We picked her up and carried her in the house. We watched her for a while, hoping that she would open her eyes and look at us. She never did. Tilly was gone. She would not play with us again. The next day Brooke and I took her to the near by vet who provided her a final resting place.

Ben grew up and started school. He is active in sports and is a faithful Sunday School member. Brooke grew up, too, and is now in school. She attends Sunday School regularly, and is studying for baptism. Brooke's hobby is playing her fiddle. She practices every day and takes part in various contests in the Valley area. I enjoyed watching Brooke and Ben grow through their babyhood years. I pray for God's continual guidance in their lives. I know we will all be together again some day in the beautiful home Jesus is preparing for us in Heaven.

For ten years I worked as a nanny giving care and guidance to the children of two families; Ben and Brooke Asbury are the children on the left. I spent six years with these children. Jessica and Jeremy Endicott are the children on the right. I have been with them for four years.

"God Bless these lovely children."

GRACE CLEMENSON

Children on Semro Street.

Nicholas Grant Dobbs, my great-grandson with mommie and daddy, Michelle and Dean Dobbs.

GRANDMOTHER'S STORIES

THE BIBLE

The Bible is God's gift to man. The Bible is a favorite book of mine, one that I keep with me and read daily. I was ten years old when I was given a New Testament Bible. This Bible I took with me through all of my teenage wanderings. I formed the habit of reading a scripture before saying my nightly prayers. This I found to be a great source of comfort to me. It is a good habit, and it will help you, too, my children. God hears every prayer and responds to every sincere desire of the heart.

The Bible consists of sixty-six books, written by many men who were prophets, inspired by God to write His word. Second Peter one twenty-one tells it clearly in these words: "Men moved by the Holy Spirit spoke from God."

Down through the ages the Bible has experienced many abuses. At one time it was imprisoned in chapels and monasteries. Priests and monks only were allowed to read its sacred words. These words were then interpreted to illiterate men according to the whims of the priests.

In later years the Bible was printed in languages common to man. It became the treasure of every home. The Word of God was restored to the people as a result of the Protestant Reformation.

Trouble arose again. The Bible became the center of controversy, when France, during the French Revolution, ordered all Bibles to be burned. Soldiers were sent out, and going from door to door breaking into homes, they confiscated the Holy Book. Great bonfires were build and God's Word was burned.

A story is told of a housewife who was mixing bread when a soldier broke into her home. She quickly took her Bible and tucked it into a pan of dough. She then put the pan into the oven. When the soldier left and the bread was done, the good woman cut open the loaf and took out her Bible. The sacred pages had suffered no harm.

The Bible has something for everyone. Do you know that you can find love stories in the Bible? The book of Ruth contains four chapters of the sweetest love story ever told.

Ruth's mother-in-law, Naomi, introduced Ruth to a relative of hers whose name was Boaz. Boaz was a wealthy land owner. Ruth was a poor girl from Moab. They fell in love. Read the story for yourself right out of the Bible.

Now turn to Genesis, chapter twenty-four. Read the story of Rebekah, who was very beautiful, and Isaac, a wealthy land owner's son. Read how they met and fell in love. The Bible says that Isaac brought Rebekah to his mother's tent, and he took Rebekah and she became his wife and he loved her.

Do you like to read stories about courageous children? Turn in your Bible to First Samuel, chapter seventeen, and read the story of David the shepherd boy, who with his sling shot, killed the giant Goliath.

Read about the boy Samuel, whose mother gave him to Eli the priest to be trained for the priesthood. God called his name three times one night while he and Eli were sleeping in their beds. God had a message for Samuel. Samuel obeyed God's call. The story is found in First Samuel, chapters one, two, and three.

Do you like war stories? Look in Judges, chapter seven, and discover how Gideon conquered Midian with only three hundred men. Each man blew on a trumpet, broke pitchers, and held up flaming torches. The three hundred all cried out together the words God gave them, "A sword for the Lord and for Gideon." All the army of the Midianites fled, crying out as they ran. God's people won the battle that day.

If you are a fisherman, turn to the New Testament. Read the story in Luke, chapater five, of Jesus' disciples who went fishing. They let down their nets according to Jesus' instructions, and caught so many fish that their nets broke. They signaled to their partners to help them. Help came and both boats were filled until they began to sink.

Jesus spent thirty years of His life preaching, teaching, and healing before He was nailed to the cross. Matthew nine, verse thirty-five, tells us that he went into all the cities and villages healing every kind of disease.

Mark chapter two tells the story of the paralytic, carried by four men to the house where Jesus was. They could not get in because of the crowd. The Bible says that they removed the roof of the house and let the paralytic down at Jesus' feet. Jesus healed a blind man by spitting in the clay and putting a mud pack on his eyes.

John chapter five tells an interesting story of a man who had been sick for thirty-eight years. He was lying on his pallet by the Pool of Bethesda, waiting for someone to help him into the water. Jesus came by and spoke to him. He was healed. He took up his pallet and walked away.

Matthew chapter five tells us that the blind received their sight, the lame walked, the lepers were cleansed, and the deaf could hear. The dead were raised up and the poor had the Gospel preached to them.

Babies! Who doesn't love to read about babies? Moses was a baby boy born to Amram and Jochebed. They lived in Egypt, and were slaves of the Egyptian king.

Moses' mother made a basket of rushes and sealed it with pitch. She put Baby Moses into the basket and hid it in the reeds near the River Nile. Read how the king's daughter came to the river to bathe. She found the baby and adopted him. This story is found in Exodus chapter one.

In Matthew chapters one and two, you will find the story of the birth of Jesus. Jesus was born in Bethlehem. Since Joseph could not find a room at the inn, Jesus was born in a manger. Herod was king in those days. He heard about the birth of Jesus. The star over the manger and the angels' visit to the shepherds announced His birth. Herod was angry. He made a decree that all boy babies born in Bethlehem should be killed. Joseph was warned by an angel in a dream to take Baby Jesus and his mother Mary and flee into Egypt. After King Herod was dead, Joseph was instructed in a dream to take Jesus and Mary to the City of Nazareth. Jesus grew up in Nazareth, working with Joseph in his carpenter shop until the time God called Him for His ministry. Jesus' work was cut short when at the age of thirty He was nailed to the cross. The cross was made of wood and was an instrument of torture which the Romans used to execute the most hardened criminals.

Jesus was crucified. He died and was buried. The grave could not hold Him. The Bible says in 1 Corinthians 15:4 that on the third day he rose again. Read the account of his death in John Chapters nineteen and twenty.

Jesus is in Heaven now, preparing a place for us there. Do you know that Jesus is coming again? "I will come again." First Thessalonians chapter four and verses fourteen through eighteen describe His coming in beautiful words you will have to read for yourself.

I know He is coming again, for I believe what the Bible says. When Jesus' disciples asked Him what the signs of His coming would be, Jesus gave them a description of the last days in the twenty-fourth chapter of Matthew.

Jesus described His coming as lightning coming from the East and flashing to the West. Revalation chapter one and verse seven says that every eye shall see Him.

The Bible is God's prophetic Word. I will close this book with these beautiful words found in II Peter 1:19 "And so we have the prophetic Word, made more sure, to which ye do well to pay attention as to a lamp shining in a dark place, until the day dawns and the daystar arises in your hearts."

God Bless You, My Children.

Marion Police Force, Marion, Iowa, about 1950.

GRANDMOTHER'S STORIES

Ellen and Verl Lindberg, 1967.

Crystal and Chuck Murphy, War years, World War II.

GRACE CLEMENSON

Ruth and Vern Johnston, Buel Manyard, Kelliher, Minnesota.

Gerhart and Grace Clemenson, 1942.

GRANDMOTHER'S STORIES

Expo 1974

GRACE CLEMENSON

Expo 1974

GRANDMOTHER'S STORIES

Crystal and Chuck Murphy
Expo 1974, Spokane, Washington.

Expo 1974, John and Joy Clemenson.

Crystal and Chuck Murphy, Grace Clemenson, Judy and Scott Clemenson, Expo 1974.

Grace Clemenson taken on Gary's acreage in Spokane, Washington, Summer of 1990.

GRANDMOTHER'S STORIES

Four Generation picture: Nicholas Grant Dobbs, Grandmother JoAnn Carlson, Great-grandmother Grace Clemenson, Mother Michelle Dobbs, taken the summer of 1989.

GRANDMOTHER'S STORIES

A

Adoption denied	17
Aladdin lamp	79
Antelope and coyotes	136
Armstrong, Gary and Becky	127
Asbury, Ben	156
Asbury, Ben and Brooke	157
Asbury, Brooke	156, 158
Aurora, Illinois	21
Aunt Either	58, funeral 59
Aunt Jenny	18
Aunt Laura	12

B

B-B in JoAnn's eye	123
Backlung, Oscar, Jr.	28, 54
Backlung, Pearl	54, 84
Backlung, Ruth and Oscar	84
Bagley, Minnesota	67
Bank Holiday	63
Baxter's Funeral Home	150
Bean's Livery barn	36
Bedbugs	79, 80
Beltrimi County, Minn.	7
Bemidji, Minn.	7, 67
Betsy (horse)	50
Bible, the	161
Bird nests	27
Bird watching	112
Blackduck	49
Blasedell Avenue	15
Bone, Dr.	46
Brenniman, Merle & Rose	86
Brettheour	148
Brunen, John	135
Buick for pennies and nickles	87
Bushy Line Road	28
Buying a house	90, 91, 100, 101

C

C.C.C. camp, 1932	74
Canadian border	26
Catching frogs	128
Catching snakes	128
Cedar Rapids, Iowa	85, 100, 115
Central High	66
Charleston, the	32
Children fighting	49
Chippewa Indian Reservation	8
Chippewa Indians	30, 81, 82
Chippewa language	8
Chipso (small dog)	80
Christmas	115
Christmas Eve	11
Christmas in a log cabin	11
Christmas presents	12
Christmas program	11
Christmas tree fire	12
Church affiliations	105
Civil War, enlistment	21
Civil War songs	21
Civilian Conservation Corps	63
Clearbrook, Minnesota	25
Clearwater Lake	75, 76, 79
Clearwater River	77
Clemenson, Alice	71
Clemenson, Betty	134
Clemenson, Betty and Clarence	88
Clemenson, Brenda	153
Clemenson, Christopher and Shaun	130
Clemenson, Dora	74
Clemenson, Gary birth of	88, 89, 90, 117
Clemenson, Gerhart Cornelius	69, 97, 137, 150, 151
Clemenson, Gerhart, police officer	99
Clemenson, Gerhart, Police work	111
Clemenson, Gerhart & Grace, wedding picture	72

Clemenson, Grace Johnson 5, baby picture 6, date of birth 7, 56, 170
Clemenson, Grace and Gerhart 88, 166
Clemenson, Gustav 71
Clemenson, Gustav & Mavis 96
Clemenson, Gunder and Millia 98
Clemenson, James 96
Clemenson, Joann, (baby picture) .... 94, birth of 92, 123
Clemenson, John & Joy 169
Clemenson, Johnny Joe, birth of 93
Clemenson, Judy & Vern 122
Clemenson, Kimberly 153
Clemenson, Patty Jo, baby picture 95
Clemenson, Patty Jo & John Brown 134
Clemenson, Phyllis 74
Clemenson, Scott 133
Clemenson, Sharon 125
Clemenson, Sharon & John 114
Clemenson, Vern, baby picture 88, birth of 92
Cleveland, Grover 22
Cold winter weather 13
Coldwell, Ann 55, 56
College Place, Washington 120
Colophon page 172
Conrad, Montana 136
Country telephone 18
Crystal 11, 12, 22, 43, 51, 52, 66, 68
Crystal and I 28
Crystal Mae (sister) 8

D

D.A.R. 15
Dailey, Miss 46
Dancing 31
Deer and Antelope 120
Diamond Point, Lake Bemidji 7
Dicky, Burl 120
Dobbs, Nicholas Grant 160
Downing, Dr. 89
Dr. Bone 15

E

Elsie 68

Emery, Miss 55
Estherville Democrat (newspaper) 25
Estherville, Iowa 23
Estherville, postmaster 22
Evans, Norma Jean 106
Expo 1974 .... 167, 168

F

Faribolt, Minn. 52, 55
Fifth birthday, my 16, 17
Fireside chats 63
First baby 83
Food stamps 97
Formal dances 55
Ford, Leighton W., chief of police 137
Ford Mercury station wagon 136
Fort Lewis 120
Fourth of July celebration 31
Funkley 32
Funkley school 52

G

Genzel, Mrs. 76
Gerhart Clemenson family 102
Gerhart's heart attack 135
Glenwood Girl's Honor Society 57
Glenwood, Minnesota 57, 65
Good Samaritan Home, Clearbook, Minn. ...25
Gonvick, Minn. 12, 51, 65, 68, street scene 78
Gonvick High School 69
Gonzaga Prep 118
Grace & Crystal 9
Grafton, Iowa 85
Grandfather Johnston 21
Grandmother's recipes 146
Grandpa Champ Maynard 25
Great Depression 63
Great Falls, Montana 136
Great Northern Railroad 120
Grone, Mrs. 39
Grove Lake 58
Grove Lake, Minnesota 25, 52, 103
Grove Lake Church 104

GRANDMOTHER'S STORIES

Grove Lake church and cemetery 59

H

Halverson, John 10
Halverson, John, with team of horses 32
Halverson, Laura 10
Halverson, Ruth 10
Hart, Guy 57, 58, 60
Haunted house 79, 80, 81
Henderson, Verner 55
Highland Fling 51
Hitchhiking home 65
Hitler 98
Home on Red Lake 34
Home on the Range (song) 121

I

Imax Theater 155
Indians 8, 30
Iowa City, Iowa 22

J

Jacobson, Mavis 131
Jewish orphanage 71
JoAnne and nap time 93
John & Grace Clemenson wedding 130
John, uncle 18
Johnston, Crystal 53, 54, 58, 61
Johnston, Elsie 53, 54, 60, 74
Johnston, George Otis 53
Johnston, George & Maynard, Edith,
  wedding, 1914 20
Johnston, Georgia 60
Johnston, Grace 52, 53, 71
Johnston Grace and Peter, home of 24
Johnston, Grace Merrill, tombstone 23
Johnston, Mary 53, 60
Johnston, Mary & George, 1918 10
Johnston, Peter, birth of . 21, law practice . 22
  death of 22
Johnston, Ruth & Vern 166

Johnston, Vern . . . . . 53, and team 66

K

Kathleen Rae, baby 83
Katz, Henry 111
Kelliher, Minn. 15, 18, 22
Kenett, Iowa 98
Kirkwood Community College 126
Knudsen, Jens & Sophia 38
Knutsen, Jimmy 84
Knutson, Ruth, hired girl 28

L

Labor union tactics 98, 99
Lake Bemiji 7
Lake Superior wilderness (honeymoon) 73
LaPlant Choate 86, 92, 98, 120
Lindberg, Ellen & Vern 165
Little Brown Church 142
Littleton, Colorado 129
Log Cabin home 19
Luger Furniture Factory 65

M

Manley, Iowa 85
Marion, Iowa 99
Marion High School 117, 120, 125
Marion, Iowa home 102
Marion, Iowa Police force 136, 164
Martin Martin's Cafe 68
Maynard, Cyrus 25
Maynard, Grandpa Champ 26
Maynard, Luthena 25
Maynard, Otis Tye 26
Merrill, George 22
Minneapolis, Minn. 15, 19, 21, 23, 28
  52, 71, 85
McGrady, Mr. 75
McGil, Dr. & Mrs. 17
McGregor, Iowa 112
Minnesota wilderness 63
Minnie Grace 7

Miss Parent (teacher) 52
Model A Ford 76, 85
Model T Ford 17, 57
Mononucleosis 119
Munsrud Farm, Gonvick, Minn. 71
Murphy, Chuck 98
Murphy, Chrystal & Chuck 165, 169
My Sweet Alice Blue Gown (song) 58

N

Nahua, Iowa 142
Nevada, Iowa 106
New Deal 63
New frame house 31
Newhard, Nancy 125
Newhard, Truman 125
Nibs (Saint Bernard dog) 28
Norden, Minn. 6, 9
Norgaard, Katherine 57
Norgaard, Mr. (school superintendent) 57
North Dakota 68
Norwegian Lutheran church, Gonvic, Minn. 150
Nurse Smith 7
Nyrenes, the 39

O

Oak Hill Cemetery, Estherville, Iowa 23
Oak Park Academy 127, 128, 132
Ogdensburg, N.Y. 21
Ogema Beach, Red Lake, Minn. . . 31, 34, 40, 49
Old Bean 35
Old Indian Trail 30
Olsen, Hulda 31
Ox and cart 10

P

Pacific Lutheran University 120
Pathfinder boys 109
Pathfinder girls 109, 110
Patton's Third Army 98
Pea Ridge, battle of 22
Peggy Jane (doll) 28

Perryville, battle of 22
Pine River, Minn. 66
Power lawn mowing business 119, 120
Protano (carpenter) 35
Protano (murderer) 35

R

Racine 12
Ralph, cousin 17
Red Lake, Shotley, Minn. 8, 14, 19, 26,
  30, 31, 49
Rheumatic fever 15, 119
Reynolds, Jim 140, 148
Rochester, Minn. 85
Rogers, the 39
Roosevelt, Franklin D. 63
Ruth 12

S

Saturday night dances 68, 69
Scarlet fever 15
Segal, Mrs. 61, 62
Seventh Day Adventist Church 105
Sheila 12
Sidewalks of New York (song) 58
Siegle, Mrs. 61
Shellsburg, Benton Co., Iowa 140
Sheriff from Bemidji 35
Shotley Brook School 42, 43
Shotley Brook school children 42
Shotley Brook store 40
Shotley, Minnesota 13
Sick papoose 8
Skunk hunting 70
Smallpox vaccination 46
South Pacific islands 98
Spokane Valley
  Seventh Day Adventist Church 152
State School for the Deaf 52, 55, 57
St. Anthony Falls 17
Stone River, battle of 22
Storm on Red Lake 27
Story City, Iowa 126

GRANDMOTHER'S STORIES

Story County Iowa barn 143
Strand, Evelyn 31
Street cars 16
Sunday School 15, 16
Sussie, cocker spaniel 151

T

Tamarack River 7, 9
Tilly (puppy) 159
Tommy (white gelding) 40, 51
Tornado 112, 113
Turkey in the Straw (tune) 51

U

Uncle Clemmy 85, 86
Uncle Ed 116
Uncle Jack 58
Uncle John 12, 18, 70
University Hospital 15
University Manor Convalescent Home 152
University of Minnesota 71
Urseth, Mrs. 39

V

Valentine Sweetheart Ball 55
Vern ...... 8, 12,   almost drowned 29

W

Walk-in-the-Wild Zoo 158
Walla Walla College 120
Wanda 12
Wapsi River 112
Wapsipinicon River 111
Wapsipenican State Park 112
WASP (aircraft carrier) 117
War time rationing 97
Wax candles 12
Weasels 8
White House lawn 63
Wild goose dinner 40
Wisconsin Dells 87
Wolves 8
Wolves, trouble with 51
Wood, Sharon, elopement with 117
Woodburning cookstove 8
Works Progress Administration 63
World War I 7
World War II 97

COLOPHON

The Grace Clemenson, GRANDMOTHER'S STORIES was printed in the workshop of Glen Adams, which is located in the quiet country village of Fairfield, southern Spokane County in Washington state and one township removed from the Idaho line. The typeface used is Garamond, a French face that has stood the test of time. The type size is 12 on 14 with a 33 pica line. Running heads and page numbers are in Baskerville Bold. The book was keyboarded by Pat Nigh using a Model 7300 Editwriter computer photosetter. Camera/darkroom was by Susan Paulson, using a DS (Japanese) camera Model 660-C, size 20x24 inches. The film was developed with a LogE 25 inch developing machine. The film was stripped by Susan Paulson who also made the printing plates. The sheets were printed by Vern Stevens using a 28 inch Heidelberg press model KORS. The sheets were folded by Garry Adams using a Baum Dial-O-Matic three stage folding machine. Assembly work was by the Ye Galleon crew. Hard case binding was by Willem Bosch of Oakesdale using a National book sewing machine. Paper copies were bound by Glen Adams and Garry Adams using a Sulby adhesive binding machine. The paper stock is seventy pound Island Offset, a Canadian sheet. This was a fun project. We had no special difficulty with the work.

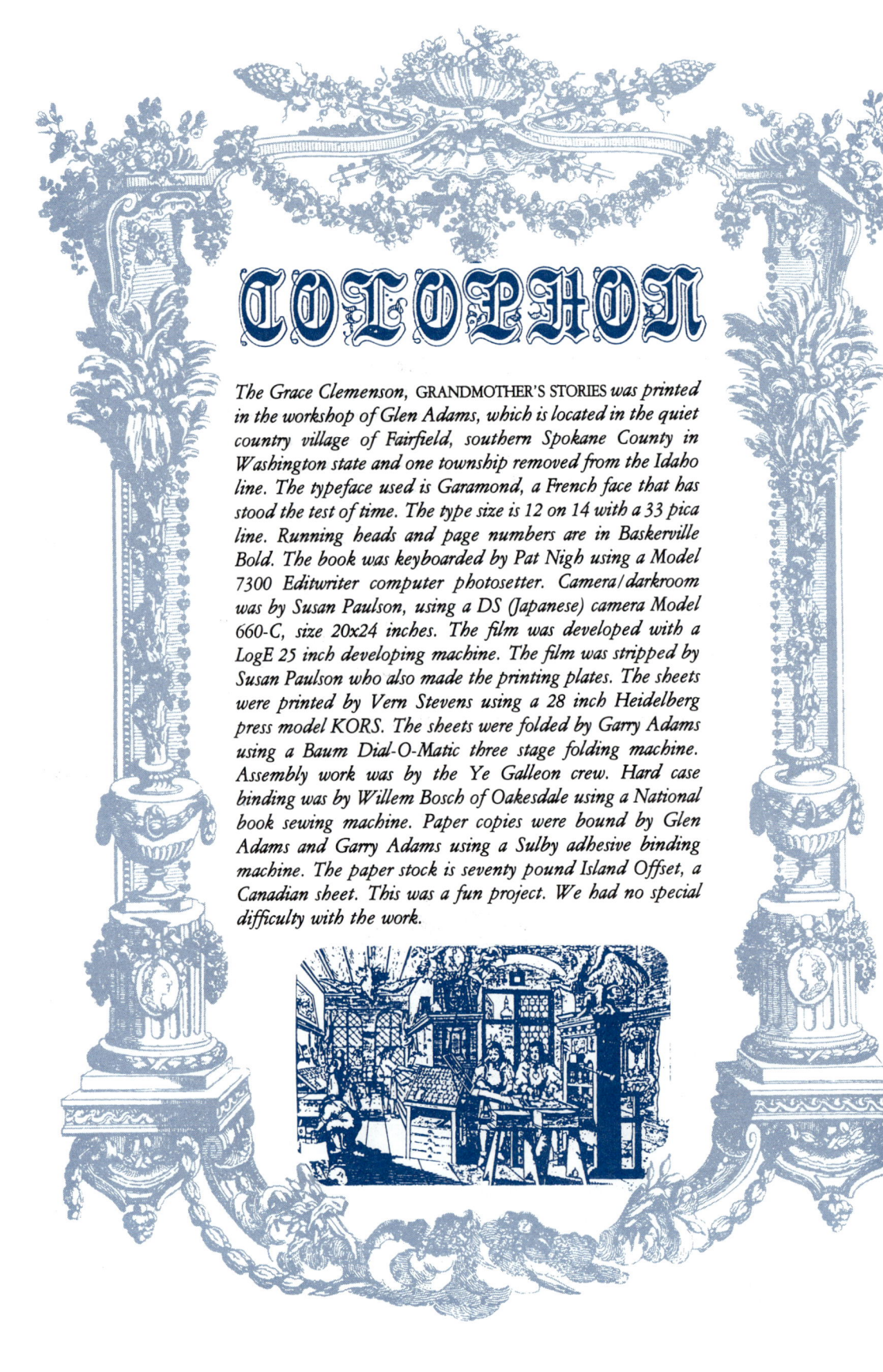